C. H. MacKintosh

THE
LIFE AND
TIMES
OF
DAVID,

King of Israel

C. H. MacKintosh

THE LIFE AND TIMES OF DAVID,

King of Israel

EMMAUS COLLEGE PRESS
(A Division of ECS Ministries)
Dubuque, Iowa

Originally Published 1851
Revised 2004

Published by:
ECS Ministries
P. O. Box 1028
Dubuque, IA 52004-1028
www.ecsministries.org

Cover Design and Typography:
Ragont Design
Barrington, Illinois

ISBN 1-59387-010-8

Unless otherwise indicated, Scripture quotations are taken
from the King James Version of the Bible.

Printed in the United States of America.
2004

CONTENTS

Prefaces   7

Introduction   13

1. David Anointed   37

2. The Valley of Elah   47

3. The Cave of Adullam   67

4. Nabal and Abigail   83

5. Ziklag   97

6. The Return of the Ark   115

7. David's House and the House of God   129

8. The Conspiracy   147

9. The Son and Last Words   169

PREFACE TO THE
ORIGINAL EDITION

In presenting to the Christian reader the following little work on "The Life and Times of David, King of Israel," I feel that there is but little demand for prefatory remarks.

Many, I am aware, whose judgment and conscience I deeply respect, disapprove of human writings on subjects connected with Sacred Scripture; and, no doubt, where such writings usurp the place of Scripture in the mind, the effect is most pernicious. But where this is not the case, I believe the Lord may make a book or tract the means of much real profit to the soul.

Were the Church, as it ought to be, gathered together in the power of the Holy Spirit, and all the members working effectually in their respective places in the body, there would be little need for such an imperfect instrumentality. But in the present scattered and divided state of Christians, when we are, of necessity, deprived of much of the viva voce instructions of our brethren, it is a mercy to receive their ministrations, even though it be only by means of "paper and ink." If we cannot have what we would, it is well to enjoy and profit by what we can; and in all things, whether we minister, or are ministered to, may we set the Lord before us, and seek to act with a single eye to His glory. This will give every one us proper sphere of action.

The present is a time of great diversity of judgment and conflict of opinion. Many simple souls know not what to think, or what to do. Various and discordant sounds fall upon the ear, and the sheep are scattered up and down in fear and uncertainty. Still, however, the circumcised ear may discern the Shepherd's voice, and this gives peace in the midst of the terrible confusion.

The history of the last few years may well teach us the difficult lesson of ceasing from man, whose breath is in his nostrils, and looking simply up to God; could we but learn this, our path, for the time to come, would be safer and happier.

May the Lord bless His own word

—C. H. M. – November 4, 1851.

PREFACE TO THE
THIRD EDITION

*M*ore than ten years have passed away since the first edition of the following work made its appearance. They have proved to be years of profound exercise of heart-searching trial and severe sifting to very many of the people of God. But, blessed be His name, the exercise, the trial, and the sifting, have, by His grace, had the effect of establishing hearts more and more in His eternal truth; of making the word of God and the name of the Lord Jesus Christ more precious; of demonstrating more clearly, that, if we want to advance in the divine life; if we desire an extension of God's kingdom within; if we would rise above the chilling atmosphere that enwraps the professing Church then, truly, we must make the Lord Christ our paramount object. We must trust in Him, wait on Him, look to Him, live for Him, and Him alone. We must get rid of more of the dross of nature and of earth, and enter more experimentally into the meaning of fellowship with Christ in death and resurrection. These are valuable results, for which we may well praise our God, and to reach which we need not regret having traveled over a rough stage of our wilderness journey.

It is an unspeakable mercy to have men and things all reduced in our thoughts to their proper dimensions: to have everything fictitious laid bare, and everything hollow made manifest; and, without doubt, a few years make a vast difference in our judgment of people and circumstances; and above all, in our judgment of self. At our first starting, there is apt to be a great deal of what may be formed *romance,* which all vanishes before the stern realities of actual life. But then we must take care that we do not exchange nature's romance, which may exhibit much that is truly generous, for nature's cold and narrow-hearted selfishness. This, alas! is too often the case.

There are two ways in which we may be affected by discovering the hollowness and vanity of men and things, namely, first, we may be driven in upon ourselves; secondly, we may be driven more closely to Christ. In the former case, the heart becomes withered and shut up; in the latter, it becomes enriched and expanded. In the former case, I become like an icicle congealed by the cold atmosphere, into which my own belief has driven me; in the latter, I get real power from God to come forth and act on the scene which had repulsed me.

It is well to ponder this distinction. We must watch against a morbid sensitiveness, which would totally unfit us for the dignified position of being "fellow-workers with God." Men and circumstances change, no doubt; but, blessed be God, we have to do with One who is "the same yesterday, to-day, and for ever." May we keep our eye steadily fixed on Him. We shall never get strength by looking at the condition of things around us.

The professing Church is in ruins; but there is something that can carry us through the ruins and that is personal devotedness to the Lord Jesus Christ. "FOLLOW THOU ME," is a simple, definite, powerful command, uttered by our blessed Lord on His way from the grave to the throne; and when this command falls on the heart, in the power of the Holy Spirit, there is that which will sustain one in the midst of the darkest apostasy, or surrounded by the solitude of a desert.

Again, "*Hold fast the form of sound words,*" is a command uttered by the apostle when he was "about to be offered up;" and when this command is applied to the conscience and understanding, by the power of the Holy Ghost, there is that which will keep one straight and steady, in the midst of the greatest confusion and inconsistency.

Nothing should hinder us in our personal devotedness to Christ, inasmuch as we can follow Him though we have not the countenance or support of another; and, further, nothing should hinder us in the maintenance of "the form of sound words;" for if the platform of public testimony were only occupied by "an elect lady and her children," they would be called upon to rise, and with a firm and vigorous hand, close the door against the introducer of unsound doctrine.

Both the above passages, taken together, would preserve us from pernicious extremes. Some contend for what they call personal devotedness, others for what they call sound doctrine; but the devotedness of the former often proves to be but the eccentricity of an un-subdued nature, or the energy of an unbroken will; and the sound doctrine of the latter often proves to be but a cold intellectual accuracy—a lifeless, sapless, uninfluential orthodoxy.

We have ever to bear in mind that "the form of sound words" is the proper foundation on which to build; and that personal devotedness is the proper superstructure to erect thereon.

The Lord grant us to know these things, in living power, by the grace of His Holy Spirit, that we may not only be in the narrow way, but move along it with an energy and a zeal which shall redound to the glory of Him who is at once the starting-post, the companion, and the goal of that way.

—C. H. M. – DUBLIN, June 1862.

INTRODUCTION
1 SAMUEL 1–15

The steps which led to the setting up of a king in Israel are easily traced, and easily accounted for, by all who have studied, with any attention, the humbling history of the human heart, either as presented in themselves or in others.

In the opening chapters of 1 Samuel, we are furnished with a most instructive and solemn picture of Israel's condition. The house of Elkanah is taken up by the sacred penman as a striking illustration of Israel after the flesh, and Israel after the Spirit. Elkanah had two wives; the name of one was Hannah, and the name of the other Peninnah. Peninnah had children, but Hannah had no children.

Thus, we have, in the domestic circle of this Ephrathite, the early scenes of Sarah and Hagar enacted over again. Hannah was the barren woman, and she was made to feel it deeply, for, "her adversary also provoked her sore, for to make her fret, because the LORD had shut up her womb."

The barren woman is always presented in Scripture as the type of nature's ruined and helpless condition. There is no ability to do anything for God; no energy to bring forth any fruit to Him, all is death and barrenness. Such is the real condition of every child of Adam. He can neither do anything for God nor for himself, as regards his eternal destiny. He is emphatically "without strength," he is "a dry tree," "a heath in the desert." Such is the lesson taught us by the barren woman.

However, the Lord caused His grace to abound over all Hannah's weakness and need, and put a song of praise into her mouth. He enabled her to say, "Mine horn is exalted in the LORD; my mouth is enlarged over mine enemies; because I rejoice in thy salvation." It is the Lord's special province to make the barren woman rejoice. He alone can say, "Sing, O barren . . . thou that didst not travail with child: for more are the children of the desolate than the children of the married wife, saith the LORD" (Isaiah 54:1).

Hannah realized this, and widowed Israel will, ere long, realize it also, "for thy Maker is thine husband; the LORD of Hosts is His name; and thy Redeemer the Holy One of Israel." The beautiful song of Hannah is the soul's thankful acknowledgment of God's actions in reference to Israel. "The LORD killeth and maketh alive: He bringeth down to the grave, and bringeth up. The LORD maketh poor and maketh rich: He bringeth low and lifteth up. He raiseth up the poor out of the dust, and lifteth up the beggar from the dunghill, to set them among princes, and to make them inherit the throne of glory." All this will be most fully exemplified in Israel in the latter day; and it is now exemplified in the person of every one whom, through grace, is raised from his ruined condition in nature, to blessedness and peace in Jesus.

The birth of Samuel filled up a great blank, not only in the heart of Hannah, but doubtless in the heart of every faithful Israelite who sighed for the true interests of the Lord's house, and the purity of the Lord's offering; both of which were alike disregarded and trampled upon by the unholy sons of Eli. In Hannah's desire for "a *man-child,*" we perceive not merely the development of the heart of a *mother,* but that of an *Israelite.* She had no doubt beheld and mourned over the ruin of everything connected with the temple of the Lord. The dimmed eye of Eli; the vile actions of Hophni and Phinehas; the fading lamp; the desecrated temple; the despised sacrifice; all conspired to tell Hannah that there was a real want, which could alone be supplied by the precious gift of a man-child from the Lord. Hence she says to her husband. "I will not go up until the child be weaned, and then I will bring him, *that he may* appear before the LORD, and there abide for ever." "Abide for ever!" Nothing short of this could satisfy the longing soul of Hannah. It was not the mere matter of wiping away her own reproach that rendered Samuel so precious in her eyes. No! she longed to see "a faithful priest," standing before the Lord; and, by faith, her eye rested on one who was to abide there for ever. Precious, elevating faith; that holy principle which lifts the soul above the depressing influence of things seen and temporal, into the light of things unseen and eternal.

In 1 Samuel chapter 3, we have the prediction of the terrible downfall of Eli's house. "And it came to pass at that time, when Eli was laid down in his place, *and his eyes began to wax dim that he could not see;* and ere the lamp of God went out in the temple of the LORD, where the ark of God was, and Samuel was laid down to sleep; *that the LORD called Samuel*" (vv. 2-4). This was very expressive; solemnly expressive. Eli's eyes dim, and the Lord's call to Samuel; in other words Eli's house is passing away, and the faithful priest is about to enter the scene.

Samuel runs to Eli, but alas! all the latter could say was "*Lie down again.*" He had no message for the child. Hoary and dim, he could spend his time in sleep and darkness, while the Lord's voice was sounding so very near him. Most solemn warning! Eli was a priest of the Lord, but he failed to walk watchfully; failed to order his house according to the testimonies of God; failed to restrain his sons; hence, we see the sad end to which he came. "And the LORD said to Samuel, Behold, I will do a thing in Israel, at which both the ears of every one that heareth it shall tingle. In that day I will perform against Eli all things that I have spoken concerning his house: when I begin, I will also make an end. For I have told him that I will judge his house forever for the iniquity which he knoweth; because his sons made themselves vile, and he restrained them not" (vv. 11-13).

"Whatsoever a man soweth," says the apostle, "that shall he also reap." How true is this in the history of every child of Adam! How peculiarly true in the history of every child of God! According to our sowing, shall be our reaping. So Eli was made to feel; and so shall the writer and the reader of this, there is much more of solemn, practical reality in this divine statement than many are apt to imagine. If we indulge in a wrong current of thought; if we adopt a wrong habit of conversation; if we pursue a wrong line of acting, we must inevitably reap the fruits of it sooner or later. The statement in the text, I need hardly say, does not by any means interfere with the eternal stability of divine grace, and the perfect acceptance of the believer, in all the acceptableness of Christ before God. This is a great foundation truth. Christ is the believer's life, and Christ is his righteousness. Hence, the ground of his peace can never be touched. He may lose the enjoyment of it, but the thing itself is beyond him. God has established it upon an indestructible basis, and before ever it can be touched, the fact of Christ's resurrection must be called in question, for clearly He could not be where He is if the believer's peace were not perfectly settled. In order to have perfect peace, I must know my perfect justification; and in order to know my perfect justification, I must know, by faith in God's word, that Christ has made a perfect atonement. This is the divine order; perfect atonement as the ground of my perfect justification; and perfect justification as the ground of my perfect peace. God has joined those three together, and let not man's unbelieving heart put them asunder. Hence, therefore, the statement in the text will not, I trust, be misunderstood or misapplied. The principle contained therein may be thus illustrated: if my child goes too near the fire, He may injure himself and grieve and displease me; but he is my child all the while. The apostolic statement is as broad as possible. "Whatever a man soweth that shall he also reap." He does not say whether it is a converted or an unconverted man; and therefore the passage should have its full application. It could not possibly touch the question of pure and absolute grace.)

May this reflection lead us to more holy watchfulness in our ways; may we be more careful to "sow to the Spirit," that so, of the Spirit, we may "reap life everlasting."

1 Samuel chapter 4 presents a humiliating picture of Israel's condition in connection with the declining house of Eli. "Now Israel went out against the Philistines to battle, and pitched beside Ebenezer: and the Philistines pitched in Aphek. And the Philistines put themselves in array against Israel: and when they joined battle, Israel was smitten before the Philistines; and they slew of the army in the field about four thousand men" (vv. 1-2). Here Israel was being made to realize the curse of a broken law. (See Deuteronomy 28:25.) They could not stand before their enemies, being weak and powerless due to their disobedience.

And observe the nature and ground of their confidence, in this their time of need and pressure. "And when the people were come into the camp, the elders of Israel said, Wherefore hath the LORD smitten us today before the Philistines? Let us fetch the Ark of the Covenant of the LORD out of Shiloh unto us, that when it cometh among us, it may save us out of the hand of our enemies" (v. 3). Alas! what a miserable ground of confidence. Not a word about *the Lord Himself*. They thought not of Him as the source of their strength; they made not Him their shield and buckler. No! they trusted in the ark; they vainly imagined that it could save them—how vain! How could it avail them anything when unaccompanied by the presence of the Lord of Hosts—the God of the armies of Israel? Impossible! But He was no longer there; He had been grieved away by their unconfessed and unjudged sin; nor could any symbol or ordinance ever take His place.

However, Israel vainly magined that the ark would do all for them, and great was their joy, though not well founded, when it made its appearance among them, accompanied not by Jehovah, but by the wicked priests, Hophni and Phinehas. "And when the ark of the covenant of the LORD came into the camp, all Israel shouted with a great shout, so that the earth rang again" (v.4). All this was very imposing; but it was hollow; their triumph was as baseless as it was unbecoming. They ought to have known much better than to make such an empty display. Their shout of triumph harmonized badly with their low moral condition in the sight of God; and yet it will ever be found that those who know least of themselves set up the highest pretensions, and assume the highest position. The Pharisee, in the gospel, looked down with an air of proud indifference on the self-abased publican; he imagined himself very high up, and the publican very low down in the scale; yet how different were God's thoughts about the two!

Thus it is, the broken and contrite heart will ever be the dwelling-place of God, who, blessed be His name, knows how to lift up and comfort every such heart as none else can do. Such is His peculiar work—the work in which He delights.

But the men of this world will always attach importance to high pretensions. They like them, and, generally speaking, give a high place in their thoughts to those who assume to be somewhat. On the other hand, they will seek to put the really self-abased man still lower. Thus, in the instructive scene before us in this chapter, the Philistines attached no small importance to the shout of the men of Israel. It was like themselves, and therefore they could apprehend and appreciate it. "And when the Philistines heard the noise of the shout, they said, What meaneth the noise of this great shout in the camp of the Hebrews? And they understood that the ark of the LORD was come into the camp. And the Philistines were afraid; for they said, God is come into the camp" (vv. 6-7). They naturally supposed that the shout of triumph was based on a reality. They did not see what was beneath the surface; they understood not the meaning of a defiled priesthood; a despised sacrifice; a desecrated temple. They beheld the outward symbol, and imagined that power accompanied it, hence their fear. How little did they know that their fear and Israel's triumph were alike groundless. "Be strong," said they, "and quit yourselves like men, O ye Philistines, that ye be not servants to the Hebrews, as they have been to you: quit yourselves *like men,* and fight" (v. 9). Here was the resource of the Philistines; "quit yourselves like men." Israel could not do this. If prevented by sin from bringing the resources of God to bear upon their circumstances, they were weaker than other men; Israel's only hope was in God, and if God were not there; if it were a mere conflict between man and man, an Israelite was no match for a Philistine. The truth of this was most fully established on the occasion to which we are referring. "The Philistines fought, and Israel was smitten" (v. 10). How else could it be? Israel could but be smitten and fly, when their shield and buckler—even God Himself—was not in their midst. They were smitten; the glory departed from them; the ark was taken and they were shorn of their strength. Their shout of triumph was exchanged for the piercing cry of sorrow. Their portion was defeat and shame, and the aged Eli, whom we may regard as the representative of the existing system of things, fell with that system, and was buried in its ruins.

1 Samuel chapters 5 and 6 embrace the period during which "Ichabod" was written upon the nation of Israel. During this time, God ceased to act publicly for Israel, and the ark of His presence was carried about from city to city of the uncircumcised Philistines. This period is full of instruction. The ark of God amongst strangers, and Israel, for the time being, set aside, are circumstances which cannot fail to interest the mind, and fix the attention of the intelligent and thoughtful student of Scripture.

"And the Philistines took the ark of God, and brought it from Ebenezer unto Ashdod. When the Philistines took the ark of God, they brought it into the house of Dagon, and set it by Dagon" (vv. 1-2). Here we are presented with the sad and humiliating result of Israel's unfaithfulness. With what a careless hand and faithless heart had they kept the ark of God, when it could ever be brought to find a lodging-place in the temple of Dagon! Truly, Israel had failed. They had let go everything. They had given up that which was most sacred, to be profaned and blasphemed by the uncircumcised.

And observe the house of Dagon was deemed sufficiently sacred for the ark of Jehovah, that ark which belonged to the holiest of all. The shadow of Dagon was to be substituted for the wings of the Cherubim, and the beams of the divine glory. Such were the thoughts of the lords of the Philistines; but not so God's thoughts. Israel had failed, no doubt, in defending the ark. They had failed to recognize the great truth that it should ever have been connected with the presence of God amongst them. All this might be true; and, moreover, the lords of the Philistines might presume to insult the sacred symbol of the divine presence by impiously associating it with Dagon their god. In a word, the Israelites might prove faithless, and the Philistines profane, but the God of Israel must ever be true to himself—ever true to His own holiness and Dagon must fall prostrate before the ark of His presence. "And when they of Ashdod, arose early on the morrow, behold, Dagon was fallen upon his face to the earth before the ark of the LORD. And they took Dagon, and set him in his place again. And when they arose early on the morrow morning, behold, Dagon was fallen upon his face to the ground before the ark of the LORD; and the head of Dagon, and both the palms of his hands, were cut off upon the threshold: only the stump of Dagon was left to him" (vv. 3-4).

Now, we can hardly conceive anything more depressing or humiliating, to all appearance, than the condition of things at this crisis, in Israel's history. They, beheld the ark snatched from their midst. They had proved themselves unfit and unable to occupy the place of God's witnesses in the view of the nations around them. And then, as to the grounds of triumph possessed by the enemies of the truth, it was enough to say; "The ark is in the house of Dagon." This was terrible, truly terrible, when looked at from one point of view; but, oh! how ineffably glorious when looked at from another! True, Israel had failed. They had let go everything that was sacred and precious. They had allowed the enemy to lay their honor in the dust, and trample on their glory; yet God was above all; beyond all; beneath all. Here was the deep source of consolation to every faithful heart. Truly, God was there, and He showed himself in wondrous power and glory. If Israel would not act in defense of God's truth, He must act Himself, and so He did. The lords of the Philistines had vanquished Israel, but the gods of the Philistines must fall prostrate before that ark, which, of old, had driven back the waters of Jordan. Here was divine triumph. In the darkness and solitude of the house of Dagon; where there was no eye to see, no ear to hear; the God of Israel was acting in defense of those great principles of truth that His Israel had so failed to maintain. Dagon fell, and, in his fall, proclaimed the honor of the God of Israel. The darkness of the moment only afforded an opportunity for the divine glory to shine out in all its brilliancy. The scene was so thoroughly emptied of the creature that the Creator could show Himself in His own proper character. "Man's extremity was God's opportunity." His failure made room for the divine faithfulness. The Philistines had proved stronger than Israel; but Jehovah was stronger than Dagon.

Now all this is replete with instruction and encouragement at a time like the present, when the people of God are so sadly declining from that high tone of devotedness and separation that ought to characterize them. We should bless the Lord for the full assurance of His faithfulness; "He cannot deny Himself" (2 Timothy 2:13). "The foundation of God standeth sure, having this seal, the Lord knoweth them that are his. And, let every one that nameth the name of Christ depart from iniquity" (2 Timothy 2:19). Hence, in darkest times, He will maintain His truth, and raise up a witness for Himself, even though it should be in the house of Dagon. Christians may depart from God's principles; but the principles remain the same; their purity, their power, their heavenly virtue, are in no wise affected by the fickleness and inconsistency of faithless professors; and, in the end, truth will triumph.

However, the effort of the Philistines to keep the ark of God amongst them proved a complete failure. They could not make Dagon and Jehovah dwell together; how awfully blasphemous the attempt "What concord hath Christ with Belial?" None whatever. The standard of God can never be lowered so as to accommodate itself to the principles that govern the men of this world; and the attempt to hold Christ with one hand and the world with the other, must issue in shame and confusion of face. Yet how many are making that effort! How many are there who seem to make it the great question how much of the world they can retain without sacrificing the name and privileges of Christians? This is a deadly evil; a fearful snare of Satan, and it may, with strict propriety, be denominated the most refined selfishness. It is bad enough for men to walk in all the lawlessness and corruption of their own hearts; but to connect their own evil with the holy name of Christ is the very climax of guilt. "Thus saith the LORD of hosts, the God of Israel, . . . Behold, ye trust in lying words, that cannot profit. Will ye steal, murder, and commit adultery, and swear falsely, and burn incense unto Baal, and walk after other gods whom ye know not, and come and stand before me in this house, which is called by my name, and say, We are delivered to do all these abominations?" (Jeremiah 7:3, 9–10) Again, we read, as one of the special characteristics of the last days, that men shall have "a form of godliness; but deny the, power thereof." The form suits the worldly heart, because it serves to keep the conscience at ease, while the heart enjoys the world in all its attractiveness. What a delusion! How needful the apostolic admonition, *"from such turn, away!"* Satan's masterpiece is the amalgamation of things apparently Christian with things decidedly unholy; he deceives more effectual by this scheme than any other, and we need more real spiritual wisdom to detect it in consequence. The Lord grant us this, for He knows how much we need it.

We come to chapter 7, passing over much that is valuable in chapters 5 and 6, and now come to dwell, for a little, upon Israel's happy restoration, in connection with the ministry of "the faithful priest."

Israel had been allowed to mourn, for many a day, the absence of the ark; their spirits drooped under the withering influence of idolatry, and at length their affections began to go out after the Lord. But, in this revival, we learn how deeply they had been sunk in death. This is always the case. When Jacob, of old, was called upon to go up to Bethel, from amid the defilement of Shechem, he had but little idea of how he and his family had become entangled in the meshes of idolatry. But the call to *"go up to Bethel,"* roused his dormant energies, quickened his conscience, and sharpened his moral perception. Hence, he says to his household, "Put away the strange gods that are among you, and be clean, and change your garments." The very idea of Bethel, as contrasted with Shechem, exerted a reviving influence on the soul of Jacob; and he, being revived himself, was enabled to lead others also in fresh power.

Thus is it with Jacob's seed, in this chapter. "And Samuel spake unto all the house of Israel, saying, If ye do return unto the LORD with all your hearts, then put away the strange gods and Ashtaroth from among you, and *prepare your hearts unto the LORD,* and serve him *only;* and he will deliver you out of the hand of the Philistines" (v. 3). We observe here what a downward course Israel had been pursuing in connection

24 + SATAN MASTERPIECE

with the house of Eli. The first step in evil is to place confidence in a form, apart from God. Apart, too, from those principles which make the form valuable. The next step is, to set up an idol. Hence, we find Israel saying of the ark, "that it may save us;" and the next thing is, "Put *away* the strange gods and Ashtaroth from among you."

Reader, is there not a solemn admonition in all this for the professing church? Truly there is. The present is, pre-eminently, a day of form without power. The spirit of cold and uninfluential formalism is moving upon the face of Christendom's troubled waters, and soon all will settle down in the death-like calm of false profession, which will only be broken in upon by "the shout of the archangel and the trump of God."

However, the attitude assumed by Israel, in the 7th chapter, forms a perfect contrast to the scene in the 4th chapter. "And Samuel said, Gather all Israel to Mizpeh, and I will pray for you unto the LORD. And they gathered together to Mizpeh, and drew water, and poured it out before the LORD, and fasted on that day, and said there, We have sinned against the LORD" (vv. 5-6). This was real work. We can say, *God is here.* There is no confidence in a mere symbol or lifeless form; there is no empty pretension, or vain assumption; no shout or baseless vaunting, all is deep and solemn reality. The earnest cry; the water poured out; the fast; the confession, all tell out the mighty change which had taken place in Israel's moral condition. They now betake themselves to the faithful priest; and, through him, to the Lord Himself. They speak not now of fetching the ark; no; their word is, "Cease not to *cry* unto the LORD our God for us, that *he* will save us out of the hand of the Philistines. And Samuel took a sucking-lamb, and offered it for a burnt offering wholly to the LORD: and Samuel cried unto the LORD for Israel; and the LORD heard him."

(vv. 8-9). Here was the source of Israel's power. The suckinglamb gave a new aspect to their circumstances; it was the turning point in their history on this occasion.

And, observe, the Philistines seem to have been in total ignorance of all that was going on between Jehovah and Israel. They, doubtless, imagined that, inasmuch as they heard no shout of triumph, the Israelites were, if possible, in a more impoverished condition than before. They do not make the earth to ring again, as in chapter 4, but, there was a silent work going on, which a Philistine's eye could not see, nor a Philistine's heart appreciate. What could a Philistine know about the penitential cry, the water poured out, or the sucking-lamb offered up? Nothing. The men of this world can only take cognizance of that which lies on the surface. The outward show; the pomp and glare; the assumption of strength and greatness in the flesh, are well understood by the world. But they know nothing of the wondrous depths of a soul exercised before God. And yet, this latter is what the Christian should most earnestly seek after. An exercised soul is most precious in the sight of God; He can dwell with such, at all times. Let us not assume to be anything, but simply take our proper place in the sight of God, and He will surely be our spring of power and energy, according to the measure of our need.

"And as Samuel was offering up the burnt offering, the Philistines drew near to battle against Israel; but the LORD thundered with a great thunder on that day upon the Philistines, and discomfited them, and they were smitten before Israel" (v.10). Such were the happy results of simple dependence upon the God of the armies of Israel; it was somewhat like the glorious display of Jehovah's power on the shores of the Red Sea. "The LORD is a man of war," when His people need Him, and their faith can use Him, in that character. When

Israel allowed Jehovah to fight for them, He was ever ready to appear with a drawn sword in His hand; but the glory must be *all* His own, Israel's shout of empty triumph must be hushed, in order that the roar of Jehovah's thunder stay be distinctly heard; and oh, how wonderfully blessed to be silent, and let Jehovah speak! What, power in His voice! Power to bring peace to His people, and to strike terror into the hearts of His enemies. "Who shall not fear thee, O LORD, and glorify thy name?"

In 1 Samuel chapter 8, we have a very marked step towards the setting up of a king in Israel. "And it came to pass, when Samuel was old, that he made his sons judges over Israel. . . . And his sons walked not in his ways, but turned aside after lucre, and took bribes, and perverted judgment" (vv. 1, 3). What a sad picture and how like man in every age. The apostle Paul says, "I know that after my departure shall griev- *Acts 20:29* ous wolves enter in among you, not sparing the flock." Israel no sooner recover from the effects of the immorality of Eli's sons, than they are made to feel the direful effects of the avarice of Samuel's sons, and thus are they hurried along the path which ended in the rejection of Jehovah, and the setting up of Saul. "When Samuel was old, *he made* his sons judges." But this was a very different thing, indeed, from God's appointment. The faithfulness of Samuel was no guarantee for his sons; just as we find in the boasted theory of apostolic succession; what kind of successors have we seen? How far have they resembled their predecessors? Paul could say, "I have coveted no man's gold;" can the so-called successors say so? Samuel could say, "Behold, here I am! witness against me before the LORD, and before His anointed: whose ox have I taken? or whose ass have I taken? or whom have I defrauded? whom have I oppressed? or of whose hand have I taken any bribe to blind mine eyes therewith?" But, alas! Samuel's sons and successors could not say this; to them, "filthy lucre" was the leading spring of action.

Now, we find, in this chapter, that Israel makes this evil of Samuel's sons the ostensible reason for asking a king. "Behold, thou art old, and thy sons walk not in thy ways; now make us a king to judge us *like all the nations.*" Fearful declension! Israel satisfied to come down to the level of the nations around, and all because Samuel was old, and his sons covetous. The Lord is shut out. Had they looked up to Him they would have had no reason for seeking to put themselves wider the guardianship of a poor mortal like themselves. But, the Lord's ability to guide and keep them was little thought of, in this entire scene; they cannot see beyond Samuel and his sons. If no help can be found from them, they must at once step down from their high elevation, and make themselves like the nations around them. The attitude of faith and dependence is too difficult to be long maintained; nothing but the actual sense of pressing need can keep us hanging upon God. In chapter 7 there was nothing about a king; God was all and in all to Israel on that occasion: but now it is not so; God is shut out, and a king is the all-engrossing object. We shall soon see the sad result of all this.

1 Samuel chapters 9 through 13 furnish us with the character of Saul, together with his anointing, and the opening of his rule. On this section I shall not dwell long, in this introduction, being merely desirous to call the reader's attention to the steps that led to the setting up of a king in Israel.

Saul was emphatically, the man after Israel's heart; he had all that the flesh could desire; "a choice young man, and a goodly; and there was not among the children of Israel a goodlier person than he; from his shoulders and upward he was higher than any of the people." This was all very imposing to those who could only look upon the outward appearance; but, what

28

a heart lay beneath this attractive exterior. Saul's whole course is marked with the deepest selfishness and pride, under the cloak of humility. When Saul hides himself, it is only that he may be brought more prominently into notice. With his heart full of the kingdom, he preserves a total silence about it to his uncle; with all his thoughts bent on the crown, he hides himself amongst the stuff; merely that he may become a more marked object, to be gazed at by the whole assembly. In fact, in every scene in which Saul moves, we recognize in him a thoroughly selfish, self-important, unsubdued man. True, the Spirit came upon him as one set apart to be an office-bearer amongst the people of God; but he was, throughout, a self-seeker, and he only used the name of God for his own ends, and the things of God as a pedestal on which to set forth his own glory. (The reader should accurately distinguish between the Holy Spirit coming; *upon* people, and the Holy Spirit dwelling: and acting in them. The statement in 1 Samuel 10:6, may present a difficulty to some minds. "The Spirit of the LORD will come *upon* thee, and thou shalt prophesy with them, and shalt be turned into another man." This is not the Spirit producing the new birth, but merely fitting Saul to be an office-bearer. Were it regeneration, it would not merely be the Spirit coming *upon,* but acting in, a man Saul the *office-bearer,* and Saul the *man,* are quite distinct, and this distinction must be maintained in reference to many of the characters both in the Old and New Testament Scriptures. An all-important difference is also to be observed in the operations of the Spirit previous and subsequent to Christ's resurrection.)

The scene at Gilgal is truly characteristic, and develops much of Saul's principle of action. Impatient to wait for God's time, he forces himself, and offers a burnt offering, and has to hear, from the lips of Samuel, these solemn words, "Thou hast done foolishly: thou hast not kept the commandment of the

LORD thy God which he commanded thee: for now would the LORD have established thy kingdom upon Israel for ever. But now thy kingdom shall not continue: the LORD hath sought him a man after his own heart, and the LORD hath commanded him to be captain over his people, because thou hath not kept that which the LORD commanded thee" (1 Samuel 13:13-14). This is just the sum of the matter, so far as Saul is concerned. "Thou hast done foolishly, thou hast not kept the commandment of the LORD . . . thy kingdom shall not continue." Solemn verities! Saul, the man after man's heart, is set aside, to make room for the man after God's heart. The children of Israel had abundant opportunity of testing the character of the man whom they had chosen to lead them forth, and fight their battles. The reed on which they had so earnestly desired to lean had broken, and was about to pierce their hand. Man's king, alas! What was he? What; could he do? Set him in an emergency, and how does he carry himself? Bustling self-importance marks all his actions. No dignity; no holy confidence in God; no acting on the broad principles of truth. Self, self, self, and that, too, in the most solemn scenes, and while apparently acting for God and His people. Such was man's king.

1 Samuel chapter 14 is a beautiful chapter furnishing a striking contrast between the efficacy of Israel's expedient, and that of the old principle of simple faith in God. Saul sits beneath a pomegranate tree, a perfect display of empty pomp without one particle of real power; while his son Jonathan, acting in the spirit of faith, is made the happy instrument of working salvation for Israel. Israel, in unbelief, had asked for a king to fight their battles, and doubtless they imagined that, when blessed with a king, no enemy could stand before them; but was it so? One word in chapter 13 gives the reply: "all the people followed him trembling" (v. 7). What a change!

How different from the mighty host who, of old, had followed Joshua into the strongholds of Canaan! And yet they now had their longed-for king before them, but God was not there, and hence their trembling. Let man have the fairest; the most imposing ordinance, without the sense of God's presence, and he is weakness itself. Let him have the presence of God, in power, and nothing can resist him. Moses had, of old, done wonders with a simple rod in his hand; but now, Israel. with the man after their own heart full in their view, could do nought but tremble before their enemies. "All the people followed him trembling." How truly humiliating! "Nay; but we will have a king over us; . . . that our king may judge us, and go out before us and fight our battles." Truly "it is better to trust *PS 118:8,9* in the LORD, than to put confidence in princes." Jonathan proved this, most blessedly. He goes up against the Philistines in the power of that word, "There is no restraint with the LORD to save by many or by few." It was "the LORD" who filled his soul, and having Him, "many or few" made no difference. Faith is never affected by circumstances; it is either God or nothing.

And mark the change which passed on Israel's circumstances, the moment that faith begins to act amongst them. The trembling was transferred from Israel to the Philistines; "and there was a trembling in the host, in the field, and among all the people; the garrison and the spoilers, they also trembled; and the earth quaked; so it was a very great trembling" (1 Samuel 14:5). Israel's star was now decidedly in the ascendant, simply because Israel was acting upon the principle of faith. Jonathan looked not to his father Saul for deliverance, but to Jehovah. Jonathon knew that He was a man of war, and on Him he leaned for the deliverance of Israel in the day of trouble. Blessed dependence! None like it. Human ordinances perish; human resources vanish away; but "they that trust in the LORD shall be as Mount Zion, which cannot be removed, but abideth for ever." "It was a very great trembling;" yes, for God was putting His terror into their hearts, and filling Israel with joy and triumph. Jonathan's faith was owned of God in the establishment of those who had previously fled from the field of conflict into the mountains. Thus it is ever; we can never walk in the power of faith without giving an impetus to others, and, on the other hand, one coward heart is sufficient to deter a great many. Moreover, unbelief always drives one from the field of service or conflict, while faith, as surely, leads one into it.

But what of Saul in all this? How did he cooperate with the man of faith ? He was perfectly incapable of any such action. He sat under the pomegranate tree, unable to inspire courage into the hearts of those who had chosen him to be their captain; and when he did venture to move, or rather to bustle forth, he could do nought but hinder the precious results of faith by his rashness and folly. But we must hasten on to the close of these introductory remarks.

1 Samuel chapter 15 presents us with the final testing and setting aside of man's king. "GO, SMITE AMALEK." This is the test that really made manifest the moral condition of Saul's heart. Had he been right before God, his sword would never have been sheathed until the seed of Amalek had ceased to breathe. But the issue proved that Saul had too much in common with Amalek to carry out the divine will in his destruction. What had Amalek done? "Thus saith the LORD of hosts, I remember that which Amalek did to Israel, how he laid wait for him in the way, when he came up from Egypt" (v. 2). In a word, Amalek stands before the spiritual mind as the first great obstacle to the progress of the redeemed from Egypt to Canaan; and we know what it is which fills a similar place in reference to those who now set out to follow the Lord Jesus.

Now, Saul had been just showing himself as a most decided obstacle in the way of the man of faith. Indeed, his entire course was one of hostility to the principles of God. How, then, could he destroy Amalek? Impossible. "He spared Agag." Just so. Saul and Agag suited each other but too well, nor had he power to execute the judgment of God on this great enemy of his people. And mark the ignorance and self-complacency of this unhappy man. "And Samuel came to Saul: and Saul said unto him, Blessed be thou of the LORD: *I have performed the commandment of the LORD*" (v. 13). How sad! Performed the commandment of the Lord, while *Agag,* king of the Amalekites, was yet alive! Oh, to what fearful lengths of vain delusion will one go when not walking uprightly before God! "What meaneth then this bleating of the sheep in my ears?" Solemn, heart searching inquiry! In vain is recourse had to the plausible matter of "*sacrifice unto the LORD.*" Miserable resource for disobedient hearts! As if the Lord would accept a sacrifice from one walking in positive rebellion against His commandment. How many since Saul's day have sought to cover a disobedient spirit with the plausible mantle of "sacrifice unto the LORD." However, Samuel's answer to Saul is of universal application, "Hath the LORD as great delight in burnt offerings and sacrifices as in obeying the voice of the LORD? Behold, to obey is better than sacrifice, and to hearken than the fat of rams. For rebellion is as the sin of witchcraft, and stubbornness is as iniquity and idolatry" (vv. 22–23). It matters not how costly the sacrifice may be, a single act of obedience to the voice of the Lord is infinitely more precious to Him. The Lord seeks not offerings, but obedience the subject heart and acquiescent spirit will glorify Him more than the cattle upon a thousand hills.

How important to have this great principle pressed home upon the conscience in this day, when so many are cloaking all sorts of disobedience with the word, Sacrifice, sacrifice! "*To*

obey is better than sacrifice.' It is far better to have the will in subjection to God than to load His altar with the costliest sacrifices. When the will is in subjection, everything else will take
its due place, but for one, whose will is in rebellion against
God, to talk of sacrificing to Him, is nothing but the most
deadly delusion. God looks not at the amount of the sacrifice, but at the spirit from which it springs. Moreover, it will
be found that all who, in Saul's spirit, speak of sacrificing
unto the Lord, have concealed beneath some selfish object,
some Agag, or the best of the sheep, or something attractive
to the flesh, which is more influential than the service or
worship of the blessed God.

May all who read these pages seek to know the real blessedness of a will entirely subject to God, for in it will be found
that blessed rest which the meek and lowly Jesus promised to
all who were heavy laden. The rest which He himself found
in being able to say, "I thank thee, O Father, ... *for so it
seemed good in thy sight.'* The restless, the ambitious Saul, knew
not this. His will did not harmonize with God's will in reference to Amalek. God had desired him to destroy Amalek, but
his heart desired to spare something which *to him,* at least,
seemed good and desirable; he was ready to carry out the
will of God in reference to all that was *"vile and refuse,"* but *he*
thought he might make some exceptions, as if the line of distinction between that which was "refuse" and that which was
"good" was to be drawn by his judgment, and not by the unerring judgment of Him who looked at Amalek from a true
point of view, and saw in Agag's most refined delicacy nothing but what was vile and refuse. He saw in him one who,
with all his delicacy, would resist Israel as strongly as ever, and
this was His ground of controversy with Amalek—a ground,
we may say, which Saul was perfectly unable to understand
or appreciate.

The close of this chapter shows us, but too plainly, the current in which Saul's thoughts and desires were flowing. He had just heard the solemn appeal of Samuel, and the denunciations of God against him, concluded with these solemn words, "the LORD hath rent the kingdom of Israel from thee, this day, and hath given it to a neighbor of thine, that is better than thou" (v. 28). These stunning words had just fallen upon his ear; yet so full was he of self, that he could say, "*honor me* now, I pray thee, before the elders of my people, and before Israel" (v. 30). This was Saul. "*The people*," said he, "spared what should have been destroyed." It was their fault, but "*honor me*." Alas, what vanity! A heart steeped in iniquity seeking honor from his fellow-worms. Rejected of God, as an office-bearer, he clings to the thought of human honor. It seems, that provided he could maintain his place in the estimation of his people, he cared but little what God thought of him. But he was rejected of God, and the kingdom torn from him; nor did it avail him much that Samuel turned again, and stood by, while Saul went through the form of worshipping the Lord, in order that he might not forfeit his place and influence amongst his people. "Then said Samuel, Bring hither to me Agag, the king of the Amalekites; and Agag came unto him delicately. And Agag said, Surely the bitterness of death is past. And Samuel said, As thy sword hath made women childless, so shall thy mother be childless among women. *And Samuel hewed Agag in pieces before the LORD in Gilgal*" (vv. 32–33). Agag's delicacy could not deceive one who was taught of God. How remarkable to find him hewing Agag in pieces *at Gilgal!* Gilgal was, the place where the reproach of Egypt was rolled away from Israel; and, in tracing their history, we find it associated with much power over evil. Here it was, then, that this Amalekite came to his end by the hand of righteous Samuel. This is most instructive. When the soul is blessed with the realization of its full deliverance from Egypt, by the power of death and resurrection, it is in the best position for obtaining victory over evil. Had Saul known anything of the spirit and principle of Gilgal, he would not have spared Agag. He was ready enough to go there to "renew the kingdom," but by no means to crush and set aside all that savored of the flesh. But Samuel, acting in the energy of the spirit of God, dealt with Agag according to the principles of truth; for it is written, "the LORD hath sworn that the LORD will have war with Amalek from generation to generation." *The king of Israel ought to have known this.*

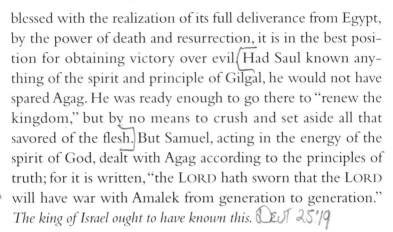

Exodus 17:16

Deut 25:19

One

DAVID
ANOINTED
1 SAMUEL 16

e now come to our theme: our rich and varied theme, the life and times of David, King of Israel. In looking through Scripture, we observe how wonderfully the blessed God has ever brought good out of evil. It was Israel's sin to reject their King Jehovah, and seek to set up a man over them; and in that man, who first wielded the scepter over them, they had learnt how vain was the help of man. The Lord was now about to bring a rich harvest of blessing to His people out of all their evil and folly.

Saul had been set aside, in the purpose of God; he had been weighed in the balance, and found wanting; his kingdom was to pass away from under his hand, and a man after God's own heart was about to be set upon the throne, to the glory of God, and the blessing of His people. 'And the LORD said unto Samuel, How long wilt thou mourn for Saul, seeing I have rejected him from reigning over Israel?" (1 Samuel 16:1). These words let us into the secret of Samuel's sorrow, in reference to Saul, during the long period of his separation from him. In the last verse of chapter 15 we read, "and Samuel came no more to see Saul until the day of his death; nevertheless Samuel mourned for Saul." This was natural. There was much that was deeply affecting to the heart in the melancholy fall of this unhappy man. He had once elicited from Israel the shout of "God save the King." Many an eye, full of enthusiasm, had doubtless rested upon "the choice young man and the goodly," and now all this was gone. Saul was rejected, and Samuel felt constrained to take a position of entire separation from him as one whom God had set aside. This was the second office-bearer whom it had been Samuel's lot to see stripped of his robes of office; he had been the bearer of heavy tidings to Eli, at the opening of his career; and now, at the close of it, he was called upon to deliver, in the ear of Saul, the announcement of the judgment of heaven against his course. However, Samuel was called to enter into the thoughts of God, in reference to Saul. "How long wilt thou mourn for Saul, seeing I have rejected him?" Communion with God will ever lead us to acquiesce in His ways. Sentimentalism may weep over fallen greatness, but faith grasps the great truth that God's unerring counsel shall stand, and He will do all His pleasure. Faith would not shed a tear over Agag, when hewed in pieces before the Lord, neither would it shed one over a rejected Saul, because it ever flows in harmony with the purpose of God, let that purpose mow down or set up whom it may. There is a wide difference between sentimentalism and faith; while the former sits down to weep, the latter arises, and fills the horn with oil. It is well to ponder this contrast. We are all too apt to be carried away by mere sentiment, which is often truly dangerous.

Indeed, inasmuch as it is of nature, it must be evil in its working, or, at least, it must flow in a current different from the thoughts of the Spirit of God. Now, the most effectual remedy against the evil working of sentiment is a strong, deep, thorough, abiding conviction of the reality of the purpose of God. In the view of this, sentimentality withers and dies, while, on the other hand, faith lives and flourishes in the atmosphere of the purpose of God. Faith says, "I thank thee, O Father," for events and circumstances, purposes and counsels, which, to all appearance, give the death blow to all the emotions of sentimentalism. This valuable principle is most impressively taught in the first verse of chapter 16, "How long wilt thou mourn? . . . Fill thine horn with oil, and go: I will send thee to Jesse the Bethlehemite: for I have provided me a king among his sons." Yes, "how long wilt thou mourn?" This is the question. Human sorrow must flow on until the heart finds repose in the rich resources of the blessed God. The varied blanks that human events leave in the heart can only be filled up by the power of faith in the precious word; "*I have provided.*" This really settles everything. This dries the tear, alleviates the sorrow, and fills the blank. The moment the spirit rests in the provision of God's love, there is a period put to all repinings. May we all know the power and varied application of this truth; may we know what it is to have our tears dried up, and our horn filled by the conviction of our Father's wise and merciful provision. This is a rare blessing; it is difficult to get completely above the region of human thought and feeling. Even a Samuel is found replying to the divine command, and manifesting a slowness to run in the way of simple obedience. The Lord said, "*Go;*" but Samuel said, "*how can I go!*" Strange inquiry! Yet how fully it develops the moral condition of the human heart. Samuel had been mourning for Saul, and now, when told to go and anoint one to fill his place, his reply is, "how can I?" Now we may be quite sure that faith never says this. There is no such word as "how" in the vocabulary of faith. No, the divine command no sooner marks out the path, than faith flies along it, with willing obedience, heedless of difficulties.

However, the Lord, in tender mercy, meets His servant in his difficulty. "And the Lord said, Take an heifer with thee, and say, I am come to sacrifice to the Lord." Thus with a full horn and a sacrifice he sets off to the city of David, where an obscure and unthought of youth tended a few sheep in the wilderness.

Amongst the sons of Jesse, there would seem to have been some very tall specimens of nature; some whom Samuel, if left to the exercise of his own judgment, would have fixed upon to succeed to the crown of Israel. "And it came to pass when they were come, that he looked upon Eliab, and said, the Lord's anointed is before Him." But it was not so. Natural attraction had nothing whatever to do with the Lord's election. He looks beneath the gilded surface of men and things, and judges according to his own unerring principles. We learn something of Eliab's haughty and self-sufficient spirit in chapter 17. But the Lord puts no confidence in the legs of a man, and thus Eliab was not His chosen vessel. It is very remarkable to find Samuel so much and so often astray in this chapter. His mourning for Saul, his refusal, or rather his hesitation, to go and anoint David. His mistake about Eliab, all shows how much astray he was as to the ways of God. How solemn is the Lord's word, "Look not on his countenance or on the height of his stature; because I have refused him: for the LORD seeth not as man seeth; for man looketh on the outward appearance, but the LORD looketh on the heart" (v. 7). This is the great difference; *"the outward appearance,"* and *"the heart."* Even Samuel was well nigh snared by the former, had not the Lord graciously interfered to teach him the value of the latter. "Look not on his countenance." Memorable words! "Then Jesse called Abinadab, and made him pass before Samuel. And he said, Neither hath the LORD chosen this. Then Jesse, made Shammah to pass by. And he said Neither hath the LORD chosen this. Again, Jesse made *seven of his* sons to pass before Samuel. And Samuel said unto Jesse, The LORD hath not chosen these" (vv. 9-10). Thus the perfection, as it were, of nature passed before the prophet, but all in vain; nature could produce nothing for God or His people. And, what is still more remarkable, Jesse thought not of David in all this. The ruddy youth was in the solitude of the wilderness, with the sheep, and came not into mind, in this review of nature's offspring. But, the eye of Jehovah was resting upon this despised youth. Beholding in him the one who was to stand in the line through which, according to the flesh, Christ should come, to occupy the throne of David, and to rule over the house of Israel forever.

Truly "God sees not as man seeth," for He "hath chosen the foolish things of the world to confound the wise; and God hath chosen the weak things of the world to confound things which are mighty; and base things of the world, and things which are despised, hath God chosen, yea, and things which are not, to bring to naught things that are; that no flesh should glory in his presence" (1 Corinthians 1:27-29.) If Eliab, or Shamunah, or Abinadab, or any one of the "seven sons" of Jesse had had the anointing oil poured upon his head, flesh might have gloried in the presence of God; but the moment David—the forgotten David—appears on the scene, we recognize in him one who would give all the glory to Him who was about to put the scepter into his hand. In a word, David stands before us as the marked type of the Lord Jesus, who, when He appeared amongst men, was despised, overlooked, and forgotten. And I may just add here, that we shall find, in ranging through David's instructive history, how strikingly he shadowed forth the true beloved of God.

"And Samuel said unto Jesse, Are here all thy children? And he said, There remaineth yet the youngest, and, behold, he keepeth the sheep. And Samuel said unto Jesse, Send and fetch him: for we will not sit down till he come hither. And he sent, and brought him in. Now he was ruddy, and withal of a beautiful countenance, and goodly to look to. And the LORD said, Arise, anoint him: FOR THIS IS HE" (vv. 11-12). "There remaineth yet the youngest." Surely he could not be the elect one, thought Jesse. Man cannot understand the ways of God. The very instrument that God is about to make use of is overlooked or despised by man. "Arise, anoint him: for this is he." Glorious words! perfect reply to the thoughts of Jesse and Samuel!

And how happy it is to note David's occupation, "Behold, he keepeth the sheep." This was afterwards referred to by the Lord, when He said to David, "I took him from the sheepfold, from following the sheep, to be ruler over my people, over Israel." Nothing can more sweetly illustrate the kingly office than the work of a shepherd. Indeed, when it is not executed in the spirit of a shepherd, it fails of its end. King David fully entered into this, as may be seen in those touching words, "*These sheep,* what have they done?" The people were the Lord's sheep, and he, as the Lord's shepherd, kept them on the mountains of Israel, just as he had kept his father's sheep in the retirement of Bethlehem. He did not alter his character when he came from the sheepfold to the throne, and exchanged the crook for the scepter. No; he was the shepherd still, and he felt himself responsible to protect the Lord's flock from the lions and bears which ever prowled around the fold. The prophetic allusion to the true David is touching and beautiful. "Therefore will I save my flock, and they shall no more be a prey; and I will judge between cattle and cattle. And I will set up one shepherd over them, and he shall feed them, even my servant David; he shall feed them, and he shall be their shepherd. And I the LORD will be their God, and my servant David a prince among them; I the LORD have spoken it." (Ezekiel 34:22-24.) And, doubtless, our Lord's words, in John 6, bade more or less reference to His shepherd character. "And this is the Father's will which hath sent me, that of all which He hath given me, I should lose nothing, but should raise it up again at the last day." This is a great principle of truth. Independent of His own personal love for the sheep, so wonderfully attested in life and in death, the Lord Jesus, in the above memorable passage, presents Himself as one responsible, voluntarily so, to the Father, to keep every member of the loved and valued flock, through all the vicissitudes of his course, and even in the matter of death itself, and present him, in resurrection glory, at the last day. Such is the Shepherd to whom a Father's hand has committed us; and, oh! How He has He provided for us for time and eternity, by placing us in such hands, the hands of an ever-living, ever-loving, all-powerful Shepherd, whose love many waters cannot quench, whose power the enemy cannot countervail. One who holds in His hand the keys of death and hell, and who has established His claim to the guardianship of the flock, by laying down His life for it. Truly we may say, "The LORD is my Shepherd, I shall not want." How can we want, while Jesus feeds us? Impossible. Our foolish hearts may often desire to feed on noxious pasture, and our Shepherd may have to prove His gracious care by denying us the use of such, but one thing is certain, that those whom Jesus feeds shall not want any *good thing.* There is something in the shepherd character that would seem to be much in harmony with the divine mind, inasmuch as we find the Father, the Son, and

Jesus Christ our Shepherd

the Spirit, all acting in that character. The 23rd Psalm may be primarily viewed as the experience of Christ, delighting in the assurance of His Father's shepherd-care. Then, in John 10, we find the Son presented as the good Shepherd. Lastly, in Acts 20 and 1 Peter 5, we find the Holy Spirit acting in that blessed capacity, by raising up and gifting for the work, the subordinate shepherds. It is edifying to mark this. It is like our God to present Himself in the most endearing relationship, and that most calculated to win our confidence and draw out our affections. Blessed be His name forever! His ways are all perfect; there is none like Him.

I would just direct the reader's attention to the contrast between the circumstances in which Samuel found David, and those in which he found Saul. He will remember that Saul was in pursuit of his father's asses, when he came in contact with Samuel. I do not interpret this fact; I merely refer to it. I believe it is expressive, in the way of evil, just as David's occupation, in the sheepfolds, was expressive of his future career, as the shepherd of Israel. When we see David tending his father's sheep in the wilderness, overlooked or thought little of in the circle of his brethren, we are led to look for something corresponding in his after-course; nor are we disappointed. Just so, when we see Saul in search of his father's asses, we are led to look for something corresponding in his character and habits afterwards. Trifling circumstances often teach a great deal. David's affectionate and tender solicitude for the Lord's flock, and forgetfulness of self, may all be traced in the circumstances in which he is introduced to our notice; and, on the other hand, Saul's ambitious, self-seeking spirit may be traced in the object of his pursuit when he came in contact with Samuel. However, I simply leave the suggestion with the reader to use as the Lord may lead him, only reminding him that nothing can be insignificant which the

Spirit has recorded concerning men who appear throughout in such marked contrast, and who each, in his way, occupied such an important place in the history of the people of God.

One can only say, blessed be the grace that took up one to be ruler over His people, who manifested those traits of character, which were most blessedly adapted to his work. "Then Samuel took the horn of oil, and anointed him in the midst of his brethren and the Spirit of the LORD came upon David from that day forward." Thus, then, David is fully before us as the Lord's anointed, and we have now to trace him in all his wanderings and vicissitudes, while rejected of man, and waiting for the kingdom.

THE VALLEY
OF ELAH
1 SAMUEL 17–18

N o sooner had the anointing oil of the Lord been poured upon David, than he was called forth to stand before King Saul, now forsaken of God, and troubled with an evil spirit. This unhappy man needed the soothing notes of David's harp to dispel the horrid influence of that spirit which now haunted him from day to day. Wretched man! sad monument of the results of a self-seeking course!

David, however, did not hesitate to take his place as *a servant,* even in the house of one who was, afterwards, to prove his most bitter enemy. It was quite the same to him where he served or what he did; he would protect his father's flocks from lions and bears, or dispel an evil spirit from Saul. In fact, from the moment David's history opens, he is seen as a servant, ready for every kind of work, and the valley of Elah furnishes a most striking manifestation of his servant character.

Saul would seem to have had little idea of who it was that stood before him, and whose music refreshed his troubled spirit; he knew not that be had in his presence the future king of Israel. "He loved him greatly; and he became his armor-bearer." The selfish Saul would gladly use the services of David in his need, though ready to shed his blood when he understood who and what he was.

But let us turn our thoughts to the deeply interesting scenes in the valley of Elah.

"Now the Philistines gathered together their armies to battle." Here now we come to something calculated to bring out the true character and worth of Saul, the man of form, and David, the man of power. It is trial that brings out the reality of a man's resources. Saul had already been proved, for "all the people had followed him trembling" (13:7), nor was he likely to prove a more soul-stirring leader on this occasion. A man, forsaken of God, and plagued by an evil spirit, was but little adapted to lead on an army to battle, or to meet, single-handed, the powerful giant of Gath.

The struggle in the valley of Elah was rendered exceedingly peculiar by the challenge, on the part of Goliath, to decide the matter by single combat; it was the very method in which an *individual* might be signalized. It was not, as in ordinary cases, army against army, but it was a question of who, throughout all the host of Israel, would venture to stand before the terrific uncircumcised foe. In fact, it is plain that the blessed God was about to make manifest again to Israel that, as a people, they were utterly powerless, and that their only deliverance, as of old, was the arm of Jehovah, who was still ready to act in His wondrous character of "a man of war," whenever faith addressed Him as such.

For forty successive days did the Philistine draw near and present himself in the view of the unhappy Saul and his awestruck army. And observe his bitter taunt; "Am not I a Philistine, and *ye servants to Saul?*" (v. 8). Alas! It was but too true; they had come down from their high elevation as servants of Jehovah to become mere servants to Saul. Samuel had forewarned them of all this, he had told them that they would become nothing more than footmen, bakers, cooks, and confectioners to their self-chosen master; and all this, instead of being able to look up to the Lord God of Israel, as their Master and King. Nothing, however, will teach man, save bitter experience; and the cutting taunts of Goliath would, no doubt, teach Israel afresh the real nature of their condition, under the crushing rule of the Philistines. "Choose you *a man* for you, and let him come down to me," said the giant. How little did he know who was about to be his antagonist. He, in all his boasted fleshly strength, vainly imagined that no Israelite could stand before him.

And here we may inquire, what of Jonathan in this entire scene? He, who had acted in such simple faith and energy in chapter 14, why was he not now ready to go forth against this champion? I doubt not, if we look particularly at his actions, we shall find that his faith was not of that simple, independent character which would carry a man on through all kinds of difficulties. The defect in his faith appears in the words, "if they say thus," etc. Faith never says "if;" it has to do only with God. When Jonathan said, "there is no restraint to the LORD," he uttered a fine principle of truth, and one that should have carried him on without an "if." Had Jonathan's soul been reposing simply in the ability of God, he would not have sought for a sign. True, the Lord graciously gave him the sign, just as he had given one to Gideon before, for he ever meets his servants in all their need. However, Jonathan does make his appearance in the valley of Elah; he had, it seems, done his work, and acted according to his measure; but, in the scene now before us, there was a demand for something far deeper than any thing Jonathan had known.

But the Lord was secretly preparing an instrument for this new and difficult work. And, my reader, may we not say it is ever thus that the blessed God acts? He trains in secret those whom He is about to use in public. He makes His servants acquainted with Himself in the secret solemnity of His sanctuary, and causes his greatness to pass in review before them, that thus they may be able to look with a steady gaze at the difficulties of their path. Thus it was with David. He had been alone with God while keeping the sheep in the wilderness; his soul had become filled with the thought of God's power; and now he makes his appearance in the valley of Elah, in all the self-renouncing dignity of a man of faith. The emptiness of man had been most fully proved, during the forty days of Goliath's haughty boasting. Saul could avail nothing. Jesse's three eldest sons could avail nothing. Even Jonathan could avail nothing; All was lost or seemed to be, when the stripling David entered the scene, clothed in the strength of Him who was about to lay in the dust the pomp and glory of the proud Philistine.

The words of Goliath were reported to David, and in them he at once recognized a blasphemous defiance of the living God. "Who," said he, "is this uncircumcised Philistine, that he should defy the armies of *the living God?*" (v. 26) David's faith recognized, in the trembling host before him, the army of the living God, and he at once made it a question between Jehovah and the Philistine. This is most instructive. No change of circumstances can ever rob the people of God of their dignity in the eye of faith. They may be brought low, in the view of man, as in Israel's case on the present occasion, but they never can lose what God has imparted; and hence David, as he beheld his poor brethren fainting in the view of their terrible enemy, was enabled to acknowledge those with whom the living God had identified Himself, and who ought not, therefore, to be defied by an uncircumcised Philistine. When faith is in exercise, it brings the soul into direct connection with the grace and faithfulness of God, and His purposes toward His people. True, Israel had brought all this sorrow and humiliation upon themselves by their unfaithfulness; it was not of the Lord that they should quail in the presence of an enemy; it was the fruit of their own doing, and faith would ever apprehend and acknowledge this. Still, the question is "who is this uncircumcised Philistine?" This is the inquiry of faith. It was not the army of Saul that filled the eye of the man of faith. No, it was the army of the living God, an army under the command of the same Captain that had led His hosts through the Red Sea, through the terrible wilderness, and through Jordan. Nothing less, nothing lower than this could satisfy faith.

But then, how little are the judgments and actions of faith understood or valued, when things get low amongst the people of God! This is very apparent on every page of Israel's history, and, we may say, on every page of the Church's history also. The path of simple, childlike faith is far removed from human sight; and if the Lord's servant sinks into a low, carnal state, they can never understand the principle of power in the soul of one really acting by faith. He will be misunderstood in various ways, and have wrong motives attributed to him; he will be accused of setting himself up, or acting willfully. All these things must be expected by one who stands in the breach, at a time when things are low. Through lack of faith in the majority, a man is left alone, and then, when he is led to act for God, he is sure to be misinterpreted.

Thus it was in David's case. Not only was he left alone in the time of difficulty, but he had to endure the taunt of the

FAITH CHALLENGE HUMAN SIGHT

flesh, administered by Eliab, his eldest brother. "And Eliab his eldest brother heard when he spake unto the men; and Eliab's anger was kindled against David, and he said, *Why* camest thou down hither? and with whom hast thou left those few sheep in the wilderness? *I know thy pride, and the naughtiness of thine heart;* for thou art come down that thou mightest see the battle" (v. 28.) This was the judgment of Eliab, in reference to the actions of David. "And David said, What have I now done? Is there not a cause?"

David was borne onward by an energy quite unknown to Eliab, nor was he careful to enter upon a defense of his course to his haughty brother. Why had not Eliab acted himself in the defense of his brethren? Why had not Abinadab or Shummah acted? Because they were faithless, simply this. Not only had those three men remained powerless, but the whole congregation had remained terror-stricken in the presence of the enemy; and now, when one appeared in their midst whom God was about to use marvelously, not one could understand him.

"And David said to Saul, Let no man's heart fail because of him; thy servant will go and fight with this Philistine" (v.32). Precious faith! No difficulty deters it—nothing stands in its way. What was the Philistine to David? Nothing. His tremendous height and formidable armor were mere circumstances; *and faith never looks at circumstances, but looks straight to God.* Had not David's soul been buoyed up by faith, he could not have uttered the words, "thy servant will go;" for, hearken to the words of him who ought to have been the first to face Israel's dreadful enemy: "And Saul said to David, Thou art not able to go against this Philistine." What language for the king of Israel! What a contrast between the man of office and the man of power! Surely Saul ought to have gone forth in the defense of the flock which had been entrusted to his care; but Saul cared not for Israel, except so far as Israel was connected with himself, and hence his exposing his person on their behalf never, we may safely say, entered his selfish heart. Not only is he unable and unwilling to act himself, but would clog the energies of one who, even now, was putting forth the precious fruits of that divine principle implanted within him, and which was about to prove him fit for the high office which the purpose of God had assigned to him, and to which His anointing oil had just dedicated him.

"*Thou* art not able." True, but Jehovah was, and David was leaning simply upon the strength of His arm. His faith laid hold of the ability of Him who had appeared to Joshua, beneath the walls of Jericho, with a sword drawn in His hand, as "Captain of the host of the LORD." David felt that Israel had not ceased to be the Lord's host, though so far sunk from what they were in Joshua's day. No; they were still the army of the Lord, and the battle was just as much the Lord's battle as when the sun and the moon were arrested in their course, in order that Joshua might execute the judgment of God upon the Canaanites. The conviction of this sustained the spirit of David, though Eliab might accuse him of pride, and Saul might talk of his want of ability.

My reader, there is nothing that can possibly give such energy and persevering power as the consciousness of acting *for God,* and that God is acting *with* us. This removes every obstacle and lifts the soul above all human influence. Let us only be fully assured that we are on the Lord's side, and that His hand is acting with us, and nothing can drive us from the path of service and testimony, conduct us where it may. "I can do all things," said the apostle, "through Christ which strengtheneth me." And again, "most gladly therefore will I rather glory in my infirmities, that the power of Christ may rest upon me." The very weakest saint can do all things, through Christ; but if the human eye rests on this weak saint it may seem like presumption to talk of doing all things. Thus, when Saul looked upon David, and compared him with Goliath, he judged rightly when he said, "Thou art not able to go against this Philistine to fight with him: for thou art but a youth, and he a man of war from his youth" (v. 33). It was a comparison of flesh with flesh, and, as such, it was quite correct. To compare a stripling with a giant would leave little room for hesitation as to the issue of the comparison. But he ought to have compared the strength of Goliath with that of the God of the armies of Israel. This was what David did. "And David said unto Saul, Thy servant kept his father's sheep, and there came a lion and a bear, and took a lamb out of the flock: and I went out after him, and smote him, and delivered it out of his mouth and when he arose against me, I caught him by his beard, and smote him, and slew him. Thy servant slew both the lion and the bear: and this uncircumcised Philistine shall be as one of them, seeing he hath defied the armies of the living God" (vv. 34–36). This was the argument of faith. The hand that had delivered from one difficulty would deliver from another. There is no "if" in all this. David did not wait for a sign; he simply said, "*thy servant will go.*" David had felt the power of God's presence with him in secret before he came forth to present himself in public as the servant of God and of Israel; and as another has remarked, David had not boasted of his triumph over the lion and the bear; no one had ever heard of it before; nor would he ever have spoken of it, doubtless, had it not been for the purpose of showing what a solid ground of confidence he had in reference to the great work on which he was about to enter. He shows that it was not in his own strength he was going forth. So was it in the matter of Paul's rapture to the third heaven; for fourteen years had that circumstance remained buried as a secret in the apostle's mind, nor would he ever have divulged it, had not the carnal reasonings of the Corinthians compelled him to do so.

Now, both these cases are full of practical instruction for us. With the majority of us there is too great a readiness to talk of our poor doings, or, at least, to think of them. The flesh is prone to glory in anything that might exalt *self;* and if the Lord, despite of the evil in us, has accomplished any little service by our instrumentality, how speedily is it communicated in a spirit of pride and self-complacency. It is all right to speak of the Lord's grace, and to have our hearts filled with thankful adoration because of it; but this is very different from boasting of things connected with self.

David, however, kept the secret of his triumph over the lion and the bear concealed in his own bosom, and did not bring it forth until the fitting occasion; nor does he, even then, speak of himself as having achieved anything, but he simply says, "*the* LORD *that delivered me* out of the paw of the lion, and out of the paw of the bear, he will deliver me out of the hand of this Philistine" (v. 37). Precious, self-renouncing faith that counts on God for everything, and trusts the flesh in nothing. Faith which brings God into every difficulty, and leads us, with deepest thankfulness, to hide self; and give Him all the glory. May our souls know more and more of this blessed faith.

But it frequently needs much spirituality to detect the vast difference between the language of faith and the language of mere commonplace and formal religiousness. Saul assumed the garb and phraseology of religiousness; we have already seen much of this in his history, and we see it in his interview with David. Mere *religiousness* and faith here shine out in marked contrast. When David had made the clear and unequivocal statement of his faith in the presence and power of Jehovah, Saul added, "Go, *and the* LORD *be with thee.*" But, how little did he know what was involved in having the Lord with him. He seemed to trust the Lord, but, *in reality,* he trusted his armor. Had he understood what he said, why think of putting on armor? "The LORD be with thee," in Saul's mouth, really meant nothing, for he had not the most distant idea of David's going simply with the Lord.

It is well to dwell upon, and distinctly point out the evil of this, the evil of using words that so far as we are concerned mean nothing, but which involve a trifling with the Lord's name and truth. How often do we speak of trusting the Lord, when, in reality, we are leaning on some circumstance, or set of circumstances. How often do we speak of living by the day in simple dependence upon God, when, if we judged the positive condition of our souls before God, we should find that we were looking to some human or earthly source of supply. This is a sad evil, and should be most carefully watched against. It was just what Saul exhibited, when, having made use of the apparently devout expression, "the LORD be with thee," he proceeded to "arm David with his armor, and he put an helmet of brass upon his head; also he armed him with a coat of mail." He had no other idea but that David was to fight in the usual way. No doubt, it was *professedly* in the name of the Lord; but he thought David *ought to use means.* But it happens that we frequently speak of using means, and really shut out God altogether. We profess to use means, in dependence upon God, and, in reality, use the mere name of God, in dependence upon the means. This is virtually, and according to the judgment of faith, to make a god of our means. What is this but plain idolatry? Had Saul more confidence in the Lord or in the armor? In the armor, no doubt. So with all who do not truly walk by faith; it is the means they lean upon, and not upon God.

We can hardly dwell upon any point in our subject more

Not Trusting God

important than that suggested by the interesting scene on which we are immediately dwelling. The man of means, and the man of faith, are really before us, and we can at once perceive how far the latter proceeds in the use of means. Means are to be used, no doubt, but only such means as are perfectly consistent with the full and blessed action of faith, and also with the untarnished glory of the God of all power and grace. Now David felt that Saul's armor and coat of mail were not such means, and he, therefore, refused them. Had he gone with them, the victory would not have been so manifestly the Lord's. But David had professed his faith in the Lord's deliverance, and not in human armor. True, we must use means; but let us take great care that our means do not shut out God. (Faith waits on God, and allows Him to use whatsoever means He *pleases*. It does not ask Him to bless our means, but lets Him use His own).

"And David girded his sword upon his armor, and he assayed to go; for he had not proved it. And David said unto Saul, I cannot go with these; for I have not proved them. And David put them off him" (v. 39). Happy deliverance from the wretched restraints of human policy! It has been observed, and most truly so, that David's trial was not when he met the giant, in actual conflict, but when he was tempted to use Saul's armor. Had the enemy succeeded in inducing him to go with that, all was gone; but, through grace, he rejected it, and thus left himself entirely in the Lord's hands, and we know what security he found there. This is what faith ever does; it leaves all to God alone. It is not the Lord and Saul's armor, but *the Lord alone*.

And, my reader, may we not apply this, with much profit to the case of a poor helpless sinner, in reference, to the forgiveness of his sins? I believe we may. Satan will tempt such a one to seek some addition to the finished work of Christ—something that will detract from the glory of the Son of God as the *only* Savior of sinners. Now, to such I would say, it matters not what you add to the work of Christ, you make it of no avail. If it might be permitted to add anything, surely circumcision would have been admitted, as being an ordinance of divine institution; yet, the Apostle says, "Behold, I Paul say unto you, that if ye be circumcised, Christ shall profit you nothing. For I testify again to every man that is circumcised, that he is a debtor to do the whole law. Christ is become of no effect unto you, whosoever of you are justified by the law; ye are fallen from grace." (Galatians 5:2-4.) In a word, then, we must have Christ *alone;* not Christ and our works, but Christ simply, for He is sufficient; we want no more, we can do with no less. We dishonor the sufficiency of His atonement if we seek to connect something of our own with it, just as David would have dishonored the Lord by going forth to meet the Philistine champion in Saul's armor. Doubtless many a so-called prudent man would have condemned what seemed to him to be the rashness and foolhardiness of the stripling; indeed, the more practiced a man was in human warfare, the more likely would he have been to condemn the course adopted by the man of faith. But what of that? David knew in whom he had believed. He knew it was not rashness that was leading him on, but simple faith in God's willingness and ability to meet him in his need. Few, perhaps, in Saul's army knew the weakness of David, as realized by himself, in that trying moment. Though all eyes were fastened upon him as one having much self-confidence, yet we know what it was that buoyed up his heart, and gave firmness to his step, as he went forth to meet the terrible foe. We know that the power of God was there just as manifestly as when the waters of the sea were divided to make a way for the ransomed to pass over; and when faith brings the power of God into action, nothing can stand in the way for a moment.

Chapter 17, verse 40 shows us David's armor. "And he took his staff in his hand, and chose him five smooth stones out of the brook, and put them in a shepherd's bag which he had, even in a scrip; and his sling was in his hand: and he drew near to the Philistine." So, we see, David did use means; but oh! What means! What contempt does David cast upon the ponderous armor of his enemy! How his sling must have contrasted with Goliath's spear like a weaver's beam! In fact, David could not have inflicted a deeper wound upon the Philistine's pride than by coming against him with such weapons. It was simply writing folly upon all his cumbersome array. Goliath felt this. "Am I a dog?" said he. It mattered not, in the judgment of faith, what he was; dog or giant; he was an enemy of the people of God, and David was meeting him with the weapons of faith. "Then said David to the Philistine, Thou comest to me with a sword, and with a spear, and with a shield: but I come to thee in the name of the LORD of Hosts, the God of the armies of Israel, whom thou hast defied. This day will the LORD deliver thee into mine hand . . . that all the earth may know that there is a God in Israel. And all this assembly shall know that *the LORD saveth not with sword and spear:* for the battle is the LORD's, and He will give you into our hands" (vv. 45-47).

Here we have the true object of the man of faith; that Israel and all the earth might have a glorious testimony to the power and presence of God in the midst of His people. This they never would have had, if David had used Saul's armor. It would not have been known that the Lord saved not by sword and spear, had David used such; his warfare would just seem like any other, but the sling and the stone left no room for doubt as to the source from whence the power of victory came. It is interesting to observe David's address to Goliath. He does not say, "*I come to thee with a sling and a stone*" No; but, *"in the name of the LORD of Hosts,"* With him, the means were nothing; God, everything.)

Faith ever honors God, and God ever honors faith. David, as has been already remarked, put himself into the hands of God, and the happy result of so doing was victory—full, glorious victory. "David prevailed over the Philistine with a sling and with a stone, and smote the Philistine, and slew him; *but there was no sword in the hand of David*" (v. 50). Magnificent triumph! Precious fruit of simple faith in God! How should it encourage the heart to cast away from it every carnal confidence, and to cling to the only true source of power. David was made the happy instrument of delivering his brethren from the galling and terrifying threats of the uncircumcised Philistine; he had come into their midst, from the retirement of a shepherd's life, unknown and despised, though the anointed king of Israel; he had gone forth single-handed, to meet the enemy of the congregation; he had laid prostrate, and made a show of him openly. All this, be it remembered, as the servant of God, and the servant of Israel, and in the energy of a faith which circumstances could not shake. It was a wondrous deliverance, gained by a single blow, no maneuvering of armies, no skill of generals and no prowess of soldiers. No; a stone from the brook, slung by a shepherd's hand, settled the whole matter. It was the victory of faith. "And when the Philistines saw that their champion was dead, they fled." How vain are those hopes that are based on the perishable resources of flesh, in its greatest apparent strength and energy! Who that saw the giant and the stripling about to engage in conflict, but would have trembled for the latter? Who would have thought that all the armor would come to nothing before a sling and a stone? Yet see the end. The champion of the Philistines fell, and, with him, all their fondly cherished hopes. "And the men of Israel and of Judah arose, and shouted, and pursued the Philistines."

Yes: they might well shout, for God was manifestly gone out before them, to deliver them from the power of their enemies. He had been working powerfully by the hand of one whom they knew not, nor recognized, as their anointed king, but whose moral grace might well attract every heart.

However, amidst the many thousands who behold the victory, we read of one whose whole soul was drawn forth in ardent affection for the victor. The most thoughtless must have been struck with admiration of the victory; and, no doubt, it affected individuals differently. We may say of it, in a certain sense, that "the thoughts of many hearts were revealed." Some would envy, some would admire; some would rest in the victory, some in the instrument; some would have their hearts drawn up to "the God of the armies of Israel," who had again come amongst them with a sword drawn in His hand. But there was one devoted heart who was powerfully attracted to *the person* of the conqueror, and this was Jonathan. "And it came to pass, when he had made an end of speaking unto Saul, that *the soul of Jonathan was knit with the soul of David*, and Jonathan loved him as his own soul" (Chapter 18:1.) No doubt Jonathan participated most fully in the joy of all, in the triumph of David; but there was more than this in it; it was not merely the triumph but the person of the triumphant one that drew out the deep and ardent affections of Jonathan's soul. Saul might selfishly seek to retain the valiant David about his person, not because of love for his person, but simply to magnify himself. Not so Jonathan; he really loved David, and truly not without reason. David had filled up a great blank in his heart, and removed a load from his spirit. A great want had been felt. The challenge of the giant had, as it was each day repeated, developed the poverty of Israel. The eye might have wandered up and down the ranks in search of one able to meet the urgent need, and wandered in vain;

there was no one. As the giant's vaunting words fell on their ears, "*all* the men of Israel, when they saw the man, fled from him, and were sore afraid." "All;" yes; all fled, when they heard his words, and saw his size. Terrible was the blank, therefore, left in the heart on this solemn occasion; and when a beloved one appeared to fill up the blank, what wonder that Jonathan's whole soul was drawn out in genuine affection for that one. And be it remembered that it was David himself; and not his work that touched Jonathan's heart. He admired his victory much, but he admired his person more. It was not merely what had been done, but the man who had done it. It is well to note this; it is well to trace its striking application to the true David. That we are warranted in making such application will not be questioned. The whole scene, from first to last, is too remarkable to admit of a question. In Goliath we behold the power of the enemy by which he held the soul in grievous bondage. From this power there was no means of deliverance within human reach. The challenge might be repeated from day to day from year to year, but all in vain. From age to age might the solemn verdict be heard throughout the myriads of Adam's fallen posterity, "it is appointed unto men once to die, but after this the judgment;" and the only response which man could yield was, like Israel's response in the valley of Elah, dismay, deep-deep dismay. "Through fear of death, all our lifetime subject to bondage." This was man's response. The need was felt-the painful void. The human heart yearned for something, and yearned in vain. The claims of justice could not be met; death and judgment frowned in the distance, and man could only tremble at the prospect. But, blessed be the God of all grace, a deliverer has appeared. One mighty to save, the Son of God, the true David the Anointed King of Israel, and of all the earth. He has met the need, filled up the blank, and satisfied the yearnings of the heart. But how? Where?

When? By His death on Calvary, in that terrible hour when all creation was made to feel the solemn reality of what was being transacted. Yes, my reader, the cross was the field where the battle was fought, and the victory won. There it was that the strong man had all his armor taken from him, and his house spoiled. There justice had its utmost claims fully satisfied; there the handwriting of ordinance, which was against us, was nailed to the tree. There, too, the curses of a broken law were forever obliterated by the blood of the Lamb, and the cries of a guilty conscience hushed by the same. "The precious blood of Christ, as of a lamb without blemish and without spot," settled everything for the believing soul. The poor trembling sinner may stand by and behold the conflict, and the glorious issue thereof—may behold all the power of the enemy laid low by one stroke of his glorious deliverer, and feel the crushing burden rolled, by the same stroke, from his struggling spirit. The tide of divine peace and joy may flow into his soul, and he may walk abroad in the full power of the emancipation purchased for him by the blood, and proclaimed to him in the gospel.

And shall not such a one, thus delivered, love *the Person* of the deliverer? Not merely the work, but the Person! How can it be otherwise? Who that has felt the real depth of his need, and groaned beneath the intolerable burden of his sins, can fail to love and adore that gracious One who has satisfied the one and removed the other? The work of Jesus, beyond a doubt, is exquisitely and infinitely precious; no human thought can ever scan its worth. Moreover, it is His work that really meets the sinner. The work of Christ introduces the soul into a position in which it can contemplate His person. In a word, then, the *work:* of the Savior is for the sinner; the *Person* of the Savior is for the saint. What He *has,* is for the former; who he *is,* is for the latter. Now, there may be much accuracy in setting

forth the work of Christ for the sinner, while the heart is cold
—the affections dull and flat—and the spiritual sensibilities
exceedingly obtuse in reference to His Person. In John chapter 6, we find a multitude of persons following the Lord Jesus
merely on selfish grounds, and He is constrained to tell them
so: "Verily, verily, I say unto you, Ye seek me, not because you
saw the miracles, but because ye did eat of the loaves, and
were filled." It was not for what He *was* they were seeking
Him, but for what He *had;* and hence, when He applies to
their hearts the searching statement, "Except ye eat the flesh
of the Son of man, and drink His blood, there is no life in
you," we read, "many of His disciples went back, and walked
no more with Him." Now, eating His flesh, and drinking His
blood, is, in other words, to have fellowship with His perfect
manhood—to drink into the power and preciousness of the
great mystery of godliness, God manifest in the flesh. The
whole gospel of John is a development of the personal glory
of the Incarnate Word, and the statement just quoted contains, as it were, the very marrow and substance of the great
doctrine as hearing upon us; yet the natural heart could not
abide it, and, therefore, many went back, and walked no more
with *Him.* The majority could not bear to have the truth concerning the Person of the Son of man pressed upon them. But
hearken to the testimony of the Church, as delivered by Peter, "Lord, to whom shall we go? thou hast the words of eternal life. And we believe and are sure that thou art the Christ,
the Son of the living God." Here we have the two things,
what He *had,* who he *was;* He had eternal life to give, and He
was the son of the living God; by the former, the sinner is
drawn to Him; by the latter, the saint is bound to Him. He not
only meets all our necessities, as sinners, by His work, but also
satisfies our affections and desires, as saints, by his Person.

All this train of thought is clearly suggested by the deeply interesting and touching interview between David and Jonathan, when all the conflict was over. The many thousands of Israel had raised the shout of triumph, and pursued the Philistines to reap the fruits of victory, while Jonathan was delighting himself in the person of the victor. "And Jonathan stripped himself of the robe that was upon him, and gave it to David, and his garments, even to his sword, and to his bow, and to his girdle" (1 Samuel 18:4). This was love, pure and simple, unaffected love, undivided occupation with an attractive object. Love strips itself for the sake of its object. David had forgotten himself, and put his life in jeopardy for God and the congregation, and now Jonathan would forget himself for David.

Reader, let us remember that love to Jesus is the spring of true Christianity. Love to Jesus makes us strip ourselves, and, we may say, that to strip self to honor Jesus is the fairest fruit of the work of God in the soul.

> *"Talk they of morals? O! thou bleeding Lamb,*
> *The great morality is love to thee."*

Very different were the feelings with which Saul regarded the person and work of David. He had not learnt to hide himself and rejoice to see the work done by another. It is a rare grace to be able to do this. We all naturally like to be or to do something—to be looked at and thought of. Thus it was with Saul. He was a self-important man, and was, therefore, little able to bear the song of the maids of Israel, "Saul hath slain his thousands, and David his ten thousand." Saul could not brook the idea of being second. He forgot how he had trembled at the voice of Goliath. He, though a thorough coward, would fair be counted brave. "And Saul eyed David from that day and forward" (v. 9), terrible eye! The eye of envy and bitter jealousy.

It requires a very simple heart and single eye to be able to rejoice as unfeignedly in the fruit of another's labors as in that of our own hands. Had the glory of God and the good of His people filled the entire compass of Saul's heart, he would not have spent a thought upon the question as to the numbers attributed to him or to David. Such, however, was not the case. He thought of his own glory. This was the secret of his envy and jealousy. O what sacred rest, what true elevation, what perfect quietness of spirit flows from self-renunciation. Such self-renunciation as results from having the heart wholly occupied with Christ! When we are honestly seeking the promotion of Christ's glory, we shall not be careful as to the instrument.

We shall have occasion to trace the development both of Jonathan's love and Saul's hatred, as we proceed in this work, and must now trace the man of faith through other scenes.

Three

THE CAVE OF
ADULLAM
1 SAMUEL 22

From amid the brilliant luster of the valley of Elah, David passed into very different scenes in the household of Saul, where envious looks, and heartless attempts upon his life, were the only returns for the soothing notes of his harp, and the valiant exploits of his sling and his sword. Saul owed his continuance on the throne, under God, to David, yet the javelin was Saul's return. But the Lord in His mercy kept His dear servant, amid all the intricacies of his extremely difficult position, "David behaved himself wisely in all his ways; and the LORD was with him. Wherefore, when Saul saw that he behaved himself very wisely, he was afraid of him. But all Israel and Judah loved David, because he went out and came in before them" (1 Samuel 18:14-16).

Thus was David, while anointed king of Israel, called upon to endure the hatred and reproach of the ruling power, though loved by all who were enabled to trace his moral worth. It was impossible that Saul and David could continue to dwell together; they were men of totally opposite principles, and, therefore, a separation should take place. David knew that he was anointed king, but, inasmuch as Saul occupied the throne, he was quite content to wait for God's time, when all that was true of him in principle should be fully actualized. Till then, the Spirit of Christ led him to take his place outside. The path of an exile—of a pilgrim and stranger—of a homeless wanderer, lay before the anointed king of Israel, and he forthwith entered upon it. His way to the throne lay through multiplied sorrows and difficulties. He, like his blessed Master and antitype, was called to suffering first, and glory afterwards. David would have served Saul to the end. He honored him as the Lord's anointed. If the moving of his finger had set him on the throne, he would not have taken advantage of it. Of this we have the fullest evidence in his having twice saved his life, when, to all appearance, the Lord had put him in his power. David waited simply upon God. Here was his strength, his elevation, his entire dependence. He could say, "My soul, wait thou *only* upon God, for my expectation is from Him." Hence we see that David was carried happily through all the snares and dangers of his path as a servant in the household and army of Saul. The Lord delivered him from every evil work, and preserved him unto that kingdom which He had prepared for him, and to which it was his purpose to raise him, "after that he had suffered a while." David had, as it were, just come from the place of secret discipline and training, to appear in the battle-field, and, having accomplished his work there, he was called to take his place again to learn some deeper lessons in the school of Christ. The Lord's lessons are often painful and difficult, because of the waywardness or indolence of our hearts; but every fresh lesson learned, every fresh principle imbibed, only fits us the more for all that is yet before us. It is truly blessed to be the disciples of Christ, and to yield ourselves to His gracious discipline and training. The end will unfold to us the blessedness of such a place. Nor need we wait for the end; even now, the soul finds it most happy to be subject, in all things, to the Master. "Come unto me, all ye that labor and are heavy laden, and I will give you rest. Take my yoke upon you, and learn of me; for I am meek and lowly in heart: and ye shall find rest unto your souls. For my yoke is easy, and my burden is light." (Matthew 11:28-30.) There are, we may say, three rests spoken of in Scripture; *first,* the rest which, as sinners, we find in the accomplished work of Christ; *second,* the present rest, which, as saints, we find in being entirely subject to the will of God. This is opposed to restlessness. *Thirdly,* the rest that remains for the people of God.

Now, David knew much of the blessedness of the second of these rests, inasmuch as he was entirely subject to the counsel and will of God, in reference to the kingdom. He was prepared to wait for God's time, being assured that it was the best and wisest time. He could say,

> *"My times are in thy hand;*
> *Father, I wish them there."*

This subjection is truly desirable; it saves one from much anxiety of heart and restlessness. When one walks in the habitual conviction that "all things are working together for good," the spirit is most wonderfully tranquilized. We shall never set about planning for ourselves, if we believe that God is planning for us; we shall be satisfied to leave all to Him. But, how often is it otherwise with us. How often do we vainly imagine that we can manage matters far better than the blessed God.

We may not say so in so many words; yet we virtually feel and act as if it were so. The Lord grant unto us a more subdued and confiding spirit. The supremacy of the will of God over that of the creature will characterize the millennial age; but the saint is called *now* to let the will of God rule him in all things.

It was this subjection of spirit that led David to give way, in the matter of the kingdom, and to take his place in the lonely cave of Adullam. He left Saul, and the kingdom, and his own destinies, in the hands of God, assured that all would yet be well. And how happy was it for him to find himself outside the unhealthy atmosphere of Saul's house, and from under the jealous glance of Saul's eye! He could breathe more freely in the cave, however it might seem in man's view, than in the household of Saul. So will it ever be; the place of separation is the freest and the happiest. The Spirit of the Lord was departed from Saul, and this was faith's warrant for separation from his person, while, at the same tine, there was the fullest subjection to his power as the king of Israel. The intelligent mind will have no difficulty in distinguishing between these two things. The separation and the subjection should both be complete. The New Testament teaches the Christian to be subject to the powers that be, but it never contemplates the idea of his being in the place of power. Hence, there are no directions for a Christian king or a Christian magistrate, though there is ample guidance for a Christian as a husband, a father, a master, or a servant. This speaks volumes.

But we must view Saul not only in a secular but also in a religious point of view; and it was in reference to the religious element in his personal character, and official capacity, that there was the greatest need for distinct and decided separation. Saul had manifested throughout a desire to rule the conscience in religious matters; witness the scene in chapter

14, where, as we have seen, spiritual energy was cramped and hindered by Saul's religious rule. Now, when such rule is set up, there is no alternative but separation. When form without power prevails, the solemn word of the Holy Spirit is, "from such turn away." Faith never stops to inquire, Whither shall I "turn"? No; the word is, "turn away." We are told what to turn away from, and we may be sure that, when we have yielded obedience to this, we shall be left at no loss as to the rest.

However, we shall see this principle in a much clearer light when we regard David in a typical point of view. In reality, David was forced into the place of separation, and thus, as one rejected of man, and anointed of God, we see him a type of Christ, in His present rejection. David was, in principle, God's king, and, as such, experienced man's hostility, being driven into exile to avoid death. The cave of Adullam became the great gathering point for all who loved David, and were wearied of the unrighteous rule of Saul. So long as David remained in the king's house, there was no call upon any one to separate; but the moment the rejected David took his place outside, no one could remain neutral; wherefore we read, "Every one that was in distress, and every one that was in debt, and every one that was discontented, gathered themselves unto him; and he became a captain over them: and there were with him about four hundred men" (1 Samuel 22:2). Here was, then, the line of distinction clearly marked. It was now David or Saul. All who loved form, loved an empty name, a powerless office, continued to adhere to Saul. But all who were dissatisfied with these things, and loved the person of God's anointed king, flocked around him in the hold. The prophet, priest, and king were there; the thoughts and sympathies of God were there, and though the company assembled there must have presented a strange appearance to the carnal and the worldly, yet it was a company gathered round the person of David, and linked with his destinies. It was composed of men, who, in their original condition, had sunk to the very lowest ebb, but who were now deriving character and distinction from their nearness and devotedness to the person of the beloved. Away from Saul—away from all that marked the day of his power—they could enjoy the sweetness of unhindered fellowship with the person of him who, though now rejected, was, ere long, to ascend the throne and wield the scepter, to the glory of God, and the joy of His people.

Reader, you may observe in David, and his despised and disreputable company, a precious sample of the true David, and those who prefer companionship with Him to all the joys, the honors, and rewards of earth. What had those who had cast in their lot with David to do with the interests of Saul? Just nothing. They had found a new object, a new center, and communion therewith separated them from all beside. Nor was their place about the person of David, at all dependent on, or connected with, what they had been. No; it mattered not what they had been; they were now the servants of David, and he was their captain. This gave them their character. They had cast in their lot with God's exile; their interest and his were identical. Happy they! Happy to escape from the rule and influence of Saul. Still more happy to find themselves in companionship with God's prophet, priest, and king. Their discontent, their distress, their debt, were all forgotten in their new circumstances. The grace of David was their present portion, the glory of David their future prospect. Just so should it be with Christians now. We have all, through grace, and the gentle leadings of the Father, found our way to Jesus—the anointed and rejected Jesus—now hidden with God. No doubt we all had our respective features of character in the days of our guilt and folly-some discontented, some in distress, all in heavy debt to God, wretched and miserable, ruined and guilty, void of everything which could attract the thoughts and affections of Christ. God has led us to the feet of His dear Son, where we have found pardon and peace through His precious blood. Jesus has removed our discontent, alleviated our distress, cancelled our debt and brought us near unto His beloved person. What return are we making for all this grace? Are we gathering, in ardent affection, round the Captain of our salvation? Are we weaned from the state of things under Saul? Are we living as those who are waiting for the moment when our David shall mount the throne? Are our affections set upon things above? "If ye then be risen with Christ," says the apostle, "seek those things which are above, where Christ sitteth on the right hand of God. Set your affliction on things above, not on things on the earth. For ye are dead, and your life is hid with Christ in God. When Christ, who is our life, shall appear, then shall ye also appear with Him in glory." (Col. 3:1-4.)

It is greatly to be feared that few really enter into the true nature and practical consequences of their position, as associated with the crucified and risen Jesus. Few really enter into the depth and meaning of our Lord's words, "they are not of the world, even as I am not of the world;" or of the Spirit's word, "the Sanctifier and the sanctified are all of one." The measure of the saint's separation from the world is nothing less than Christ's; i.e., the principle of it; looked at practically, alas! it is quite another thing; but in principle, there is no difference. It is of vast importance to enforce this principle just now. The actual standing, calling and hopes of the Church are but very imperfectly understood. The feeblest believer in Jesus is, in God's view, as separate from all belonging to earth as Jesus. It is not a matter of attainment but of positive, simple, abstract standing: not an object after which we must strive, but a point from which we must start. Many have been led astray by the idea that

73

we must work up to a heavenly position by shaking off the things of earth. This is to begin at the wrong end. It is the same error, only in reference to another department of truth, as to assert that we must work up to a condition of justification, by mortifying the sins of the flesh. Now, we do not mortify self in *order to be* justified, but *because we are* justified; yea, dead and risen with Christ. In like manner, we do not put away things of earth, in order to become heavenly, but because we are so. We have the heavenly calling independent of everything, and in proportion as we enter into it, will we be separate from earth. But to make our standing the result of conduct, instead of conduct the result of standing, is a grievous error. Ask a saint, really intelligent as to the heavenly calling, to give a reason for his standing apart from the present system of things, what will be his reply? Will he tell you that he does so in order to become heavenly? No. Will he tell you that it is because the present system is under judgment? No. No doubt it is under judgment, but this is not the true ground of separation. What then? "We are dead, and our life is hid with Christ in God." "They are not of the world, even as I am not of the world." "Holy brethren, partakers of the heavenly calling." Here we have the grand reason for the saint's present separation from the world. It does not matter what the world is, be it good or bad; he is not *of* it, though *in* it, as the place of his daily toil, conflict, and discipline.

Christians should ponder well the heavenly calling; it is the only thing that will give full deliverance from the power and influence of worldliness. Men may seek *abstraction* from the world in various ways, but there is only one in which to attain *separation* from it. Again, men may seek to render themselves *unearthly* in various ways; there is only one way in which we can become really *heavenly*. Abstraction is not separation; nor is unearthliness to be mistaken for heavenliness. The monastic

ATTENTION TO ARE
HEAVENLY CALL

system illustrates very fully the distinction between these things. A monk is unearthly, in a certain sense, but by no means heavenly; He is unnatural, but by no means spiritual; he is abstracted from the world, but by no means separated from it.

Now, the heavenly calling enables a man to see his entire separation from, and elevation above, the world, in virtue of *what* Christ is, and *where* He is. The heart instructed by the Holy Spirit, as to the meaning of Hebrews 2:11, knows the secret of his deliverance from the principles, habits, pursuits, feelings, and tendencies, of this present age. The Lord Jesus has taken His place on high, as head of the body, the Church; and the Holy Spirit has come down to lead all the foreknown and predestinated members of the body into living fellowship with the living Head, now rejected from earth, and hidden with God. Hence in the gospel, as preached by Paul, the remission of sins is inseparably connected with the heavenly calling, inasmuch as he preached the unity of the one body on earth with its Head in heaven. He preached justification, not merely as an abstract thing, but as the result of what the Church is, as one with Jesus, who is now at the right hand of God, Head over all things to His Church, angels and principalities being made subject to Him. Paul preached remission of sins, no doubt, but he preached it with all the fullness, depth, power, and energy, which the doctrine of the Church imparts to it.

The epistle to the Ephesians teaches us not only that God can forgive sinners, but far more than this, it unfolds to us the wondrous truth, that believers are members of the body of Christ; "for we," says the apostle, "are members of His body, of His flesh, and of His bones." Again, " But God, Who is rich in mercy, for His great love wherewith He loved us, even when we were dead in sins, hath quickened us together with Christ (by grace ye are saved); and hath raised us up together, and made us sit together in heavenly places in Christ Jesus." Again,

"Christ also loved the church, and gave himself for it; that He might sanctify and cleanse it with the washing of water by the word. That He might present it to himself a glorious church, not having spot, or wrinkle, or any such thing; but that it should be holy and without blemish." These passages present far more than mere remission of sins. To be the bride of the Lamb is a very much higher, very much more glorious thing, than merely to have our sins forgiven.

> *"Yet 'tis not that we know the joy*
> *Of cancell'd sin alone,*
> *But, happier far, thy saints are call'd*
> *To share thy glorious throne."*

Just so, the blessed God has gone beyond all man's thoughts in His mode of dealing with the Church. He has called us, not only to walk here below in the full sense of His pardoning love, but also to know the love of Christ to His body, the Church, and the high and holy dignity of that Church, its seated in the heavenlies.

My reader may, perhaps, inquire, what has the Cave of Adullam to do with the Church's place in the heavens? It has to do with it only so for as it illustrates the present place of rejection into which Christ has entered, and which all must know who enjoy fellowship with Him. We are not to suppose, for a moment, that David's men knew anything about the heavenly calling, as the Church now knows it. We may frequently discover, in Old Testament Scripture, foreshadowings of the heavenly calling, in the characters, walk, and circumstances of certain prominent persons that are introduced to our notice; but this is a very different thing, indeed, from asserting that such persons actually knew the heavenly calling.

The fact is, the heavenly calling, properly speaking, was not known until the Lord Jesus took his seat on high, and the Holy Spirit came down to baptize believers, Jew and Gentile, into one body; then the heavenly calling was developed in all its power and fullness. This truth was peculiarly committed to Paul; it was an essential part of the mystery committed to him, and was embodied in these words, "why persecutest thou *me*" Saul was persecuting the saints, and the Lord Jesus appeared to him in heavenly glory, and told him that these saints were part of Himself. Henceforth this became Paul's great thesis; in it he found involved the unity of the Church, and the heavenly calling of the Church.

And let the reader observe, that all this was not merely an admission of the Gentile into the Jewish fold. (I would say a word here, on the opening verses of John 10. The Lord Jesus presented Himself at the door of the Jewish fold, and having obtained entrance, called out His sheep that were therein, and then He says, "Other Sheep I have, which are not of this fold; them also I must bring, and they shall hear my voice; and there shall be one fold [flock] and one Shepherd." It is strange that the translators should have rendered this "one fold," when the Greek word for fold actually occurs in the same verse. Nor is the distinction unimportant. A fold conveys the idea of certain arrangements entered into for the purpose of keeping sheep on earth; hence the word is properly applied to the Jewish economy. Now, however, it is no longer a fold—an earthly arrangement—a penning up of sheep here below; all that has passed away. The heavenly Shepherd has called forth His Jewish sheep from the earthly fold, and His Gentile sheep from the dark mountains of this wide world, and having made of the two one new flock, He has put it into the Father's hand. Thus we see the difference between the words fold and flock. But if any should be disposed to differ from the view here stated, I can only say that the Holy Spirit did not intend that the different Greek words should both convey the same idea). No, it was simply taking both Jew and Gentile out of their circumstances in nature, and setting them down in new circumstances—new to both. The work of the cross was needful to break down the middle wall of partition, and to make of two, one new man, i.e., to make of Jew and Gentile a new heavenly man, to be totally separated from earth and the things thereof. The present place of Christ in the heavens is connected with the rejection of Israel and the earth, during what is called the Church period, and this serves to bring out, still more fully and distinctly, the heavenly character of the Church of God. She lies completely outside the range of earth; she has nothing to do with "this present age"; she belongs entirely to heaven, though manifesting, or at least, called to manifest, on earth, the living energy of the Holy Spirit who dwells in her.

Thus, as David's men were withdrawn from all connection with Saul's system, by virtue of their association with him, so all those, who are led by the Spirit to know their oneness with the absent Jesus, must feel themselves dissociated from present things, by reason of that blessed oneness.

Hence, if you ask a heavenly man why he does not mix himself up with the plans and pursuits of this age, his reply will be, because Christ is at the right hand of God, and I am identified with Him. The true way in which to test the various objects presented to the saint, is simply to ask, could the Lord Jesus engage in them? If not, we can have nothing whatever to do with them. All who understand the true nature of the heavenly calling will walk in separation from the world; but those who do not, will just take their portion here, and live as others.

Many, alas, are satisfied with the mere knowledge of the forgiveness of sins, and never think of going further. They have

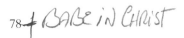

passed through the Red Sea, it may be, but manifest no desire to cross the Jordan, and eat the old corn of the land of promise. Just as it was in the day of David's rejection; there were multitudes of Israelites who did not cast in their lot with him; but this did not hinder their being Israelites. It was one thing to be an Israelite; it was another thing to be with David in the hold. Even Jonathan was not there; he still adhered to the old system of things. He, though loving David as his own soul, lived and died in companionship with Saul. True, he occasionally ventured to speak *for* David, and sought his company when he could. He had stripped himself to clothe David, but he did not cast in his lot *with* him. And, consequently, when the names and the deeds of David's worthies are heralded by the Holy Spirit, we look in vain for the name of the affectionate Jonathan; when the devoted companions of David's exile were mustering round his throne, and basking in the sunshine of his royal countenance, poor Jonathan was mingled with the dust, having ingloriously fallen, on Mount Gilboa, by the hands of the uncircumcised Philistines.

Oh! that all who profess to love the Lord Jesus Christ may seek a more decided identification with Him in this the time of His rejection. The citizens *of this world* have sent a message after him, saying, "we will not have this man to reign over us;" and shall we go and associate ourselves with those citizens to forward their Christ-rejecting plans? God forbid. May our hearts be with Him where He is. May we know the hallowed fellowship of the Cave of Adullam, where the Prophet, Priest, and King, are to be found, embodied in the beloved Person of Him who loved us, and washed us from our sins, in His own blood. We cannot walk with Saul and David at the same time; we cannot hold Christ and the world; we must take our choice. The Lord grant us grace to reject the evil and choose the good, remembering the solemn words of the apostle; "This is a faithful saying; for if we be dead *with Him,* we shall also live *with Him;* if we suffer, we shall also reign with Him; if we deny Him, He also will deny us." This is the time of suffering, the time for enduring afflictions and hardness; we must wait for the time of rest. David's men were called, by reason of their association with him, to undergo much toil and fatigue, but love made all light and easy to them; and their names and exploits were all faithfully remembered, and minutely recorded when David was at rest in his kingdom. None were forgotten. The twenty-third chapter of 2 Samuel will furnish the reader with the precious catalogue, and will, no doubt, lead his mind onward to the time when the Lord Christ shall reward His faithful servants, those who from love to His person, and by the energy of His Spirit, have performed acts of service for Him in the time of His rejection. These acts may not be seen, known, or thought of by men; but Jesus knows them, and will publicly declare them from the throne of His glory.

Who would ever have known the acts of David's worthies, if the Holy Spirit had not recorded them? Who would have known of the three who drew water from the well of Bethlehem? Who would have known of the slaying of a lion in a pit, in the time of snow? Just so now, many a heart throbs with love to the Person of the Savior, unknown to all; and many a hand may he stretched forth in service to Him, unobserved by every human eye. It is sweet to think it is so, especially in an age of cold formality like the present; sweet to think of those who love the Lord Jesus Christ in sincerity. Some there are, who are not only indifferent to His beloved Person, but who even go so far as to rob Him of His dignity, and make Him little better than Elias, or one of the prophets. But, my reader, we shall not dwell upon these; we have, thank God, a happier theme, and we shall, with His help, pursue it. We shall think of those valued men who jeopardized their lives for the sake of their captain, and who, the instant he uttered his desire, were ready, at all cost, to gratify it. Love never pauses to calculate. It was quite sufficient for those worthies to know that David longed for a drink from the well of Bethlehem—the drink must be procured at all cost; "And these three mighty men brake through the host of the Philistines, and drew water out, of the well of Bethlehem, that was by the gate, and took it and brought it to David: nevertheless he would not drink thereof, but poured it out unto the LORD."

There is something peculiarly touching and beautiful in the above scene, whether we contemplate the act of the three mighty men in procuring the water for David, or David's act in pouring it out to the Lord. It is evident that David discerned, in an act of such uncommon devotedness, a sacrifice which none but the Lord Himself could duly appreciate. The odor of such a sacrifice was far too fragrant for him to interrupt it in its ascent to the throne of the God of Israel. Wherefore he, very properly and very gracefully, allows it to pass him by, in order that it might go up to the One who alone was worthy to receive it, or able to appreciate it. All this reminds us, forcibly, of that beautiful compendium of Christian devotedness set forth in Philippians 2:17-18, "Yea, and if I be poured out upon the sacrifice and service of your faith, I joy and rejoice with you all; for this cause do ye also joy and rejoice with me" In this passage, the apostle represents the Philippians saints, in their character as priests, presenting a "sacrifice" and performing a priestly ministration to God; and such was the intensity of his self-forgetting devotedness, that he could rejoice in his being poured out as a drink offering upon their sacrifice, so that all might ascend, in fragrant odor, to God. The Philippians laid a sacrifice on God's, altar, and the apostle was poured out upon it, and all went up to God as an odor of sweet smell. It mattered not who put the sacrifice on the altar, or who was poured out thereon, provided that God received what was acceptable to Him. This, truly, is a divine model for Christian devotedness. Would that we had grace to form our ways according to it. There would, then, be far less of "*my* sayings," and "*my* doings," and "*my* goings." It would be our joy, wherever we saw one or another laying a sacrifice on the altar of God, to allow ourselves to be poured out as a drink offering thereon, to the glory of God and the common joy of his saints.

Lovely scene! Sweet sample of what the Church ought to be! Loving not her life unto the death, for Christ's sake. Oh! that the Holy Spirit may kindle within us a flame of ardent love to the Person of Jesus—may He unfold to our souls more of the divine excellencies of His Person, that we may know Him to be the fairest among ten thousand, and altogether lovely, and be able to say with a true worthy, "Yea, doubtless, and I count all things but loss, for the excellency of the knowledge of Christ Jesus my Lord; for whom I have suffered the loss of all things, and do count them but dung, that I may win Christ." (Philippians 3:8.)

NABAL AND
ABIGAIL
I SAMUEL 25

It is interesting to observe, as we pass from stage to stage of David's history, how different individuals were affected toward his person, and the consequent position assumed in reference to him. It required an energy of faith to discern, in the despised outcast, the future king of Israel. To all who judged according to human principles, Saul would seem to have been badly treated by David, and David's course, in wandering about the country, would appear wholly unwarrantable. In this chapter we are presented with two most striking examples of persons thus variously affected in reference to David's person and career.

"There was a man in Maon, whose possessions were in Carmel; and the man was very great, and he had three thousand sheep, and a thousand goats: and he was shearing his sheep in Carmel, the name of the man was Nabal" (1 Samuel 25:2). This

Nabal was an Israelite, and he appears in marked contrast with David, who, though anointed king of Israel, had nowhere to lay his head, but was a wanderer from mountain to mountain, and from cave to cave. Nabal was a selfish man, and had no sympathy with David. If he had blessings, he had them for himself; if he was "great," he had no idea of sharing his greatness with any one else, and least of all with David and his companions.

"And David heard *in the wilderness* that Nabal did shear his sheep. And David sent out ten young men, and David said to the young men, Get you up to Carmel, and go to Nabal, and greet him in my name" (vv. 4-5). David was in the wilderness; this was his place. Nabal was surrounded by all the comforts of life. The former owed all his sorrows and privations to what he was; the latter owed all his possessions and enjoyments to what he was. Now, we generally find that where advantages are derived from religious distinction and profession, much selfishness exists. The profession of truth, if not connected with self-denial, will be connected with positive self-indulgence; and hence we may observe, at the present day, a most determined spirit of worldliness, connected with the very highest profession of truth. This is a grievous evil. The apostle was made to feel the anguish of it, even in his time. "Many," says he, "walk, of whom I have told you often, and now tell you, even weeping, that they are *the enemies of the cross of Christ: whose end is destruction, whose God is their belly, and whose glory is in their shame, who mind earthly things.*" (Philippians 3:18-19.) Observe, they are the enemies of the cross of Christ. They do not throw off all semblance of Christianity; far from it, "Many *walk.*" This expression shows a measure of profession. The persons here pictured would, doubtless, be much offended, were any to refuse them the appellation of Christians; but then they do not want to take up the cross; they desire not practical

identification with a crucified Christ; whatever amount of
professed Christianity can be had apart from all self-denial, is
welcome to them, but not a single jot beyond this. "Their God
is their belly, and they mind earthly things." How many must
plead guilty to the charge of minding earthly things. It is easy
to make a profession of the religion of Christ while the Person of Christ is unknown, and the cross of Christ is hated. It
is easy to take up the name of Jesus into the lips, and connect
it with all that personal care, self-indulgence, and love of the
world, which the human heart knows so well how to estimate. All this find its full illustration in the person of the
churlish Nabal, who, having shut himself up in the midst of
his luxuries and wealth, cared not for God's anointed, nor fill,
for him in the season of his painful exile and sojourn in the
wilderness.

What was his reply to David's touching appeal? "Who is
David? and who is the son of Jesse? there be many servants
now-a-days that break away every man from his master. Shall
I then take my bread, and my water, and my flesh that I have
killed for my shearers, and give it unto men whom I know
not whence they be?" (vv. 10-11). Here was the secret of this
worldly man's estrangement of heart; *he did not know him;* had
he known him, it would have been a very different matter:
but he neither knew who he was nor whence he was; he did
not know that he was railing on the Lord's anointed, and cast-
ing from him, in his selfish folly, the privilege of ministering
to the need of the future king of Israel.

The moral of all this is deeply instructive. It demands a real
energy of faith to enable any one to discern the Person of
Christ, and cleave fully to Him in the time of His rejection. It
is one thing to be a Christian, as people say, and another thing
to confess Christ before men. Indeed, one can hardly find
anything more selfish than that condition of heart that would

FALSE PROFESS CHRISTIANS

lead us to take all that Jesus has to give, and yield Him nothing in return. Provided I am saved, all the rest is unessential." This is the secret thought of many a heart, and if thrown into a more honest form would be this, "If I am sure of salvation, it matters little about the glory of Christ." This was just Nabal's mode of thought; he reaped all the advantage he could from David; but the moment David put in his claim for sympathy and aid, his worldly spirit developed itself. "One of the young men told Abigail, Nabal's wife, saying, Behold, David sent messengers out of the wilderness, to salute our master; and he railed on them. But the men were very good unto us, and we were not hurt, neither missed we anything, as long as we were conversant with them, when we were in the fields: They were a wall unto us both by night and by day, all the while we were with them keeping the sheep" (vv. 14–16). This was all very well. Nabal could well understand the value of David's *protection,* though he cared not for David's *person.* So long as David's men were, a wall to his possessions, he would tolerate them; but when they would become a burden, they were rejected, and railed upon.

Now, as might be expected, Nabal's action was directly contrary to Scripture, as his spirit was decidedly contrary to the spirit of its Divine Author. It is written in Deuteronomy chapter 15, verses 7 to 9, "If there be among you a poor man of one of thy brethren within any of thy gates, in thy land which the LORD thy God giveth thee, thou shalt not harden thine heart, nor shut thine hand from thy poor brother: but thou shalt open thine hand wide unto him, and shall surely lend him sufficient for his need, in that which he wanteth. Beware that there be not a thought in thy wicked heart, saying, The seventh year, the year of release is at hand; and thine eye be evil against thy poor brother, and thou givest him naught; and he cry unto the LORD against thee, and it be sin unto thee." Precious grace! How like God! How unlike Nabal! Grace would keep the heart open wide to every object of need; whereas selfishness would close it against every applicant. Nabal ought to have obeyed the word, independently of his knowledge of David; but his selfishness was of too deep a character to allow of his obedience to the Lord's word, or his love to the Lord's anointed.

However, Nabal's selfishness led to very important results; it led, in David's case, to the exhibition of much that was calculated to humble him in the presence of God. He is here seen to come down from the high elevation that usually characterized him, through the grace of God. No doubt, it was deeply trying to meet with such base ingratitude from one to whom he had been a wall of defense; it was galling, too, to be reproached on the very ground of those circumstances into which faithfulness had called him, to be accused of breaking away from his master at the very time that he was being hunted as a partridge through the mountains. All this was hard to bear and David gives expression to words that would not bear the examination of the sanctuary. "*Gird ye on every man, his sword,*" was not just the language that we should have expected from one who had hitherto walked in such a meek and gentle spirit. The scripture just quoted presents the resource of the poor brother, "cry unto the Lord," not to draw his sword for revenge. Nabal's selfishness could never have been remedied by the sword of David, nor would faith ever have adopted such a course. We do not find David acting thus in reference to Saul; he left him entirely to God, and even when induced to cut off the skirt of his robe, his heart smote him. Why did he not act thus toward Nabal? Because he was not in communion; he was off his guard, and the enemy took advantage of him. Nature will ever lead us to vindicate ourselves, and resent every injury. The heart will secretly murmur, "he had no

right to treat me thus; I really cannot bear it, nor do I think I ought to do so." This may be so, but the man of faith at once rises above all such things; he sees God in everything; the jealousy of Saul, the folly of Nabal, all is looked at as coming from the hand of God, and met in the secret of His holy presence. The instrument is nothing to faith; God is in all. This gives real power to move on through all sorts of circumstances. If we do not trace God in everything, we shall be constantly ensnared.

We shall have occasion, as we proceed with our subject, to trace this principle more fully, and shall now turn to another character introduced to our notice in this instructive chapter. This is Abigail, the wife of Nabal, "a woman of good understanding, and of a beautiful countenance." A noble testimony, surely, and one that shows that grace can manifest itself in the most untoward circumstances. The house of the churlish Nabal must have been a withering scene to one like Abigail; but she waited on God, and, as we shall see, was not disappointed.

The case of this remarkable woman is full of encouragement and instruction to all who may find themselves cramped and hindered by unavoidable; connections and associations. To all such the history of Abigail simply says, Be patient, wait on God, do not suppose yourself void of all opportunity for testimony. The Lord may be much glorified by meek subjection, and will, assuredly, give relief and victory in the end. True, some may have to reproach themselves for having formed such connections, or entered into such associations; but, even so, if the folly and evil are really felt, confessed, and judged before God, and the soul brought into an attitude of thorough subduedness, the end will be blessing and peace. In Abigail we see one who was actually used to correct no less a personage than David himself. It may be that her course, up to the time at which the sacred historian introduces her to our notice, had been marked by much that was painful and trying; indeed, it could hardly have been otherwise, associated with such an one as Nabal. Time, however, brought to light the grace that was in her. She had suffered in obscurity, and was now about to be raised to an unusually high elevation. Few had seen her patient service and testimony; but many beheld her exaltation. The burden that she had borne in secret was about to drop off before many witnesses. The preciousness of Abigail's service did not consist in her having saved Nabal from the sword of David, but in keeping David from drawing the sword at all. "Now David had said, Surely in vain have I kept all that this fellow hath in the wilderness, so that nothing was missed of all that pertained unto him; and he hath requited me evil for good" (v. 21). This was terrible. David was rashly taking himself out of the place of dependence, the only happy, the only holy place. Nor was it on behalf of the congregation of the Lord. No, it was to avenge himself on one who had treated him badly. Sad mistake! Happy was it for him, that there was an Abigail in the house of Nabal who was about to be used of God to keep him from answering a fool according to his folly. This was just what the enemy desired. Nabal's selfishness was used by Satan to ensnare David, and Abigail was the Lord's instrument to deliver him. It is well when the man of God can detect Satan's working; to be able so to do, he must be much in the presence of God, for there alone can he find light and spiritual power to enable him to cope with such a foe. When out of communion, the soul becomes distracted by looking at secondary causes, and subordinate agents, just as David was distracted by looking at Nabal. Had he paused to view the matter calmly, before God, we should not have had such words as, "In vain have I kept all that this fellow hath in the wilderness;" he would have passed on, and left "this fellow" to himself. Faith imparts real dignity to the character, and superiority over the petty circumstances of this transient scene. Those who know themselves as pilgrims and strangers, will remember that the sorrows as well as the joys of this life are transient, and they will not be inordinately affected by either the one or the other. "Passing away," is written on everything; the man of faith must, therefore, look upward and onward.

Now Abigail by the grace of God delivered David from the unhappy influence of the *present,* by leading his soul onward into the *future:* we learn this from her exquisite address to him. "And when Abigail saw David, she hasted, and lighted off the ass, and fell before David on her face, and bowed herself to the ground, and fell at his feet, and said, Upon me, my lord, upon me let this iniquity be: and let thine handmaid, I pray thee, speak in thine audience, and hear the words of thine handmaid. Let not my lord, I pray thee, regard this man of Belial, even Nabal: for as his name is, so is he; Nabal is his name, and folly is with him: but I thine handmaid saw not the young men of my lord whom thou didst send. Now therefore, my lord, as the LORD liveth, and as thy soul liveth, seeing the LORD hath withholden thee from coming to shed blood, and from avenging thyself *with thine own hand,* now let thine enemies, and they that seek evil to my lord, be as Nabal; . . . for *the LORD will certainly make my lord a sure house; because my lord fighteth the battles of the LORD,* and evil hath not been found in thee all thy days. Yet a man is risen to pursue thee, and to seek thy soul; *but the soul of my lord shall be bound in the bundle of life with the LORD thy God;* and the souls of thine enemies, them shall He sling out, as out of the middle of a sling. And it shall come to pass, *when the LORD shall have done to my lord according to all the good that He hath spoken concerning thee, and shall have appointed thee ruler over Israel,* that this shall be no grief unto thee, nor offence of heart unto my lord, either that thou hast shed blood causeless, or that my lord hath avenged himself: but when the LORD shall have dealt well with my lord, then remember thine handmaid'] (vv. 23-26, 28-31). We can hardly conceive anything more touching than this address; every point in it was calculated to touch the heart. She presents to him the evil of seeking to avenge himself; the weakness and folly of the object of his revenge. She reminds him of his proper occupation, "fighting *the LORD's battles.*" This must have brought home to his heart the humiliating circumstances in which Abigail met him, even rushing on to fight *his own* battle.

However, the reader will perceive that the leading point in this address is the special reference to the future. "The LORD *will* certainly make my lord a sure house." "The soul of my lord *shall* be bound in the bundle of life with the LORD thy God." "When the LORD *shall* have done to my lord," etc.; "and *shall* have appointed thee ruler over Israel." All these allusions to David's future blessing and glory were eminently calculated to withdraw his heart from his present grievance. The sure house, the bundle of life, and the kingdom, were far better than Nabal's flocks and herds; and in the view of these glories, David could well afford to leave him to his portion, and his portion to him. To the heir of a kingdom, a few sheep could have but little attraction; and one, who knew that he had the anointing oil of the Lord upon his head, might easily bear to be called a runaway servant. All these things Abigail knew— knew as matters of faith. She knew David, and knew his high destinies. By faith she recognized in the despised outcast the future king of Israel. Nabal knew not David. He was a man of the world, swallowed up with present things. With him there was nothing more important, nothing more influential, than "*my* bread, *my* flesh, *my* shearers;" it was all self; there was no room for David or his claims. This might be expected from such an one; but surely it was not for David to go down from his elevation to grapple with a poor worldling about his perishable possessions. No, the kingdom should have filled his eye, and engaged his thoughts, and lifted his spirit above all lower influences. Look at the Master Himself, as he stood at the bar of a poor worm; the creation of His own hand—how did He conduct Himself? Did he call upon his little band of followers to gird on every man his sword? Did He say of the man who dared to sit as His judge, "In vain have I imparted unto this fellow all he is, and all he has?" No, He looked above and beyond Pilate, Herod, the chief priests, and scribes. He could say, "the cup which MY FATHER hath given me, shall I not drink it?" This kept His spirit tranquil, while, at the same time, He could look forward into the future, and say, "HEREAFTER shall ye see the Son of Man sitting on the right hand of power, and coming in the clouds of heaven." here was real power over present things. The millennial kingdom, with all its untold joys, with all its heights and depths of glory, glistened in the distance, with everlasting light and brilliancy, and the eye of the Man of sorrows rested upon it, in that dark hour, when the scoffs and sneers, the taunts and reproaches of guilty sinners were falling upon His blessed Person.

Dear Christian reader, this is our model; thus ought we to meet the trials and difficulties, the reproach and desertion of this present time. We should view *all* in the light of "*hereafter.*" "Our light affliction," says an eminent sufferer, "which is but for a moment, worketh for us a far more exceeding and eternal weight of glory." Again, "but the God of all grace, who hath called us to his eternal glory by Christ Jesus, after ye have suffered a while, make you perfect, stablish, strengthen, settle you." "O fools, and slow of heart to believe all that the prophets have spoken! Ought not Christ to have suffered these things, and to enter into his *glory?*" Yes; suffering must come first and glory afterwards; and any one who, by his own hand, would seek to take off the edge of present suffering and reproach, proves that. the kingdom is not filling the whole compass of his soul—that *now* is more influential with him than "*hereafter.*"

How we ought to bless our God for having opened such a vista of glory, in the ages to come! How it enables us to tread, with a buoyant step, our rugged path through the wilderness! How it lifts us above the things that engross the children of this world!

> "*We're not of the world, which fadeth away,*
> *We're not of the night, but children of day;*
> *The chains that once bound us by Jesus are riven,*
> *We're strangers on earth, and our home is in heaven*"

May we prove the sacred reality of this, more and more, as we pass along through "this dark vale of tears."Truly the heart would sink, and the spirit faint, were we not sustained by hope —even the hope of glory, which, thank God, maketh not ashamed.

In pursuing the narrative of David and Abigail a little further, we have a still more striking example of the vast difference between the child of nature and the child of faith. Abigail returned from her interview with David, and found Nabal "very drunken: wherefore she told him nothing, less or more, until the morning light. But it came to pass in the morning, when the wine was gone out of Nabal, and his wife had told him these things, that his heart died within him, and he became as a stone. And it came to pass, about ten days after, that the LORD smote Nabal, that he died" (vv. 37-38). What a sad picture of a man of the world! Sunk in intoxication during the night, and when the morning dawned, struck with terror, pierced by the arrow of death. How solemnly like the multitudes whom the

Wine, Drunkard End +*Next pages*

enemy has succeeded, in every age, in alluring and intoxicating with the perishing joys of it world which lies under the
curse of God, and awaits the fire of His judgement. "They that
sleep, sleep in the night, and they that be drunken are drunken
in the night;" but, the morning is at hand, when the wine (apt
symbol of this world's joy) shall have altogether evaporated,
the feverish excitement in which Satan now involves the spirits
of the men of this world shall have calmed down, and then
comes the stern reality of an eternity of misery in company
with Satan and his angels. Nabal did not even meet David face
to face; yet the very thought of his avenging sword filled his
soul with deadly fear. How much more terrible will it be to
meet the gaze of a despised and rejected Jesus! Then the Abi-
gails and the Nabals will find their respective places; those who
had known and loved the true David, and those who had not.
God, in His mercy, grant that my reader may be amongst the
happy number of the former.

I would only observe, further, that the interesting narrative of this chapter gives us a striking picture of the Church and
the world, as a whole; the one united to the king, and associated with him in his glory; the other plunged in irretrievable
ruin. "Seeing then that all these things shall be dissolved, what
manner of persons ought ye to be in all holy conversation and
godliness, looking for and hasting unto the coming of the day
of God, wherein the heavens being on fire shall be dissolved,
and the elements shall melt with fervent heat? Nevertheless
we, according to his promise, look for new heavens and a new
earth, wherein dwelleth righteousness. Wherefore, beloved,
seeing that ye look for such things, be diligent, that ye may be
found of him in peace, without spot, and blameless" (2 Peter
3:11-14). Such are the soul-stirring, momentous facts presented to us throughout the book of God, in order to detach
our hearts from present things, and bind them in genuine

affection to those objects and prospects which stand connected with the person of the Son of God. Nor will anything else, except the deep and positive conviction of the reality of these things, produce such effects. We know the intoxicating power of this worlds schemes and operations; we know how the human heart is borne away, as upon the surface of a rapid current, when such things are presented, schemes of improvement, commercial operations, political movements; aye, and religious movements, too—all these things produce upon the human mind an effect similar to that produced by Nabal's wine, so that it is almost useless to announce the stern facts presented in the above solemn quotation. Still, however, they must be announced, must be reiterated, "and so much the more, as we see the day approaching." "The day of the Lord will come as a thief in the night." "All these things shall be dissolved." "The heavens being on fire shall be dissolved, and the elements shall melt with fervent heat; the earth also, and the works that are therein, shall be burned up." Such is the prospect presented to all who, like Nabal, surcharged with "surfeiting, and drunkenness, and cares of this life," have rejected the claims and appeals of Jesus. The world is being prepared for the introduction of that one who, by the energy of Satan, will head up all its institutions, embody all its principles and concentrate all its energies. Let but the last elect one be gathered out, the last member be incorporated into the body of Christ by the quickening energy of the Holy Spirit, the last stone be set in its appointed place in the temple of God, and then shall the salt be removed, which now preserves the world from corruption; the barrier presented by the presence of the Holy Spirit in the Church shall be taken out of the way, and then comes first the lawless one on the stage of this world, "whom the Lord shall consume with the Spirit of His mouth, and destroy with the brightness of His coming. Even Him whose coming is after the working of Satan with all power, and signs, and lying wonders, and with all deceivableness of unrighteousness in them that perish (because they received not the love of the truth, that they might be saved.)"

Surely these things ought to check the career of the men of this world, and lead them, with solemnized minds, to "consider their latter end." "The long-suffering of our Lord is salvation." Precious word! Most precious! But let it not be abused; let it not be mistaken for "*slackness.*" The Lord waits to be gracious to *sinners,* not to connive at *sin.*

However, as has been already observed, it is almost useless to speak to men about the *future* who are wholly engrossed with the *present.*

Blessed be God, there are some who have ears to hear the testimony about the kindness and grace of Jesus, as well as about His coming judgment. Thus it was with Abigail; she believed the truth about David, and acted accordingly; and all, who believe the truth about Jesus, will be found separating themselves diligently from this present world.

Five

ZIKLAG

I SAMUEL 28–30

In dwelling upon a history such as that now before us, which, of necessity, presents much failure and infirmity, it is well for us to keep in memory what we ourselves are, lest we be found pointing out the lapses of others in a spirit of self-complacency. The divine penman has set before us, with unflinching fidelity, all the imperfections of those whose history He records. His object is to present God to the soul in all the fullness and variety of His resources, and in all His competency to meet the helpless sinner in his very deepest need. He has not written the history of angels, but of men "of like passions with us." And this is what makes Old Testament narratives so exceedingly instructive to us. We are presented with facts that speak to the heart. We are conducted through scenes and circumstances that unfold to us, with touching simplicity, the hidden springs of our nature, and also the hidden springs of grace. We learn that man is the same in every age; in Eden, in Canaan, in the Church, in millennial glory, he is proved to be made of the same humbling materials; but we learn also, for our joy and encouragement, that God is "the same yesterday, today, and for ever," "Patient, gracious, powerful, holy," patient, to bear with our grievous and manifold provocations; gracious, to blot out our oft-repeated sins, and restore our wandering souls; powerful, to deliver us out of Satan's entangling snares, and from the energy of nature and the world; holy, to execute judgment in His house, and to chasten His sons, that they may be partakers of His holiness. Such is the God with whom we have to do; and we see the wondrous unfolding of His character in the deeply-interesting sketches with which Old Testament history abounds, and in none, perhaps, more than in that now before us. Few characters exhibit more variety of experience than David. He truly knew the depth and heights that mark the course of the man of faith. At one moment, we find him giving forth from his harp the most sublime strains; at another, pouring forth the sorrows of a defiled conscience, and a wounded spirit. This variety of experience rendered David a fit subject for illustrating the varied grace of God. It is ever thus. The poor prodigal would never have known such high communion, had he not known the humiliating depths of the far country. The grace which decked him in the best robe would not have shone so brightly, had he not been clad in filthy rags. God's grace is magnified by man's ruin; and the more keenly the ruin is felt, the more highly the grace is valued. The elder brother never got a kid that he might make merry with his friends; and why? Because he imagined he had earned it, "Lo," says he, "these many years do I serve thee, neither transgressed I at any time thy commandment." Vain man! How could he expect the ring, the robe, or the fatted calf? Had he obtained them, they would have been but the trappings of self-righteousness, and not the ornaments with which grace decks the believing sinner.

Thus was it with Saul and David. Saul never knew his need as David knew it, nor have we any record of such flagrant sins, in his case; at least, that man would pronounce flagrant. Saul was the outwardly moral and religious man, but, withal, a self-righteous man; hence we have such expressions as these, "I have performed the commandment of the LORD," "Yea, I have obeyed the voice of the LORD, and have gone the way which the LORD sent me." How could this man value grace? Impossible. A heart unbroken, a conscience unconvinced, can never enter into the meaning of the term Grace. How different it was with David! He felt his sins, groaned under them, confessed them, judged them, in the presence of God whose grace had blotted them all out forever. There is a great difference between a man ignorant of his sins, and walking in self-complacency, and one deeply conscious of his sins, yet happy, in the full forgiveness of them.

The above train of thought introduces us to the circumstances connected with David in Ziklag of the Philistines; circumstances that fully manifest human infirmity, and divine grace and mercy.

"And David said *in his heart,* I shall now perish one day by the hand of Saul: there is nothing better for me than that I should speedily escape into the land of the Philistines" (1 Samuel 27:1). This was David's second visit to the land of the Philistines. In chapter 21 we read, "and David arose and fled that day for fear of Saul, and went to Achish the king of Gath." Here we find David really taking himself out of the hands of God, and putting himself into the hands of Achish. He leaves the place of dependence, and goes into the very midst of the enemies of God and of Israel. And, be it remarked, he has in his hand the very sword of the Philistine champion. Nor is it to act in his true character as the servant of God; this would have been happy, indeed; but no; he goes to act the madman, in the presence of those before whom he had so recently acted as the champion of Israel. "The servants of Achish said unto him, Is not this David, the king of the land? Did they not sing one to another of him in dances, saying, Saul hath slain his thousands, and David his ten thousands?" (21:11). The Philistines recognized David's true character as "king of the land," the slayer of ten thousands. They imagined that he could not possibly act otherwise than as their enemy. Little were they able to enter into the moral condition of his soul at that extraordinary stage of his history. Little did they think that the slayer of Goliath had fled to them for protection from the hand of Saul. The world cannot understand the fluctuations of the life of faith. Who that had seen David in the valley of Elah could ever suppose that he would so soon fear to avow, with boldness, the results of that faith with which God had endowed him? Who could have thought that with Goliath's sword in his hand, he could tremble to avow himself the victor of Goliath? Yet so it was. "David laid up these words in his heart, and was sore afraid of Achish, the king of Gath. And he changed his behavior before them, and feigned himself mad in their hands and scrabbled on the doors of the gate, and let his spittle fall down upon his beard" (21:12-13.) Thus must it ever be, when a saint deserts the path of simple dependence upon God, and strangership in the world. The "behavior" must be "changed," the real character abandoned, and instead a course is adopted which is marked by positive deceit before God, and folly before the world. This is most sorrowful. A saint should always maintain his dignity—the dignity that flows from the consciousness of the presence of God. But the moment faith gives way, the power of testimony is gone, and the man of faith is despised as a "madman." When David "said in his heart, I shall now perish one day by the hand of Saul," he forsook the only path of real power. Had he continued as a homeless wanderer through the mountains, he would never have presented such a melancholy picture, in the view of the servants of Achish, he would never have been pronounced a madman. Achish would not have dared to call David by such a name in the valley of Elah, no, nor in the Cave of Adullam. But, David had put himself into the power of this stranger, and therefore he should either suffer for his past faithfulness, or give all up, and pretend to be a fool in their eyes. They rightly judged him to be the king of the land, but he, afraid of the consequences of maintaining such a high dignity, denied his kingship, and became a fool. How frequently may we trace the working of this same evil in the walk of Christians! How frequently may we see a man who, by his past actions in the energy of the Spirit of God, has attained a very high position in the thoughts, not only of his brethren, but even of the children of this world, and yet, when such an one gets out of communion, he is really afraid to maintain his position, and, at the very moment when those without are looking only for an unbending and unqualified testimony against their ways, he changes his behavior, and instead of being esteemed and reverenced, he is actually despised. We should most carefully guard against this; it can only be effectively avoided by walking in the full and blessed consciousness of God's sufficiency. So long as we feel that God is sufficient for *all* our need, we are entirely independent of the world; if it be not thus with us, we shall just compromise the truth of God, and deny our real character as heavenly men.

How completely must David have lost the sense of God's sufficiency when he could say, "There is *nothing better* for me than that I should speedily escape into the land of the Philistines." Nothing better for a man of faith than to go back to the world for refuge! Strange confession! The confession of one who had allowed circumstances to come between his soul and God. When we slip off the narrow path of faith, we are liable to run into the wildest extremes; and nothing can more forcibly exhibit the contrast between one looking at God, and one looking at circumstance, than David in the valley of Elah, and David scrabbling on the doors of the Philistine king. The contrast is full of solemn instruction and warning. It is well calculated to teach us what we are, and how little the best of us can be depended upon. My dear Christian reader, what are we? Poor, failing, stumbling creatures, prone, at every turn in our path, to wander into error and evil—prone to forsake the Rock of Ages, and lean upon the broken reeds of the world, to forsake the fountain of living waters, and hew out for ourselves broken cisterns that can hold no water. Truly we have need, deep need, to walk humbly, watchfully, and prayerfully, before our God —deep need to utter David's own prayer, continually, 'Uphold me according unto thy word, that I may live: and let me not be ashamed of my hope. Hold thou me up, and I shall be safe: and I will have respect unto thy statutes continually' (Psalm 119:116-117). We need to have our feet made as hinds' feet, so that we may walk on the high and slippery places through which our path lies. Nothing short of divine grace can enable us to pursue a course of steady devotedness: for, if left to ourselves, there is no extreme of evil into which we may not run. They alone are safe whom God keeps in the hollow of His hand. Truly happy is it for us to have to do with one who is able to bear with us in all our waywardness, and able also to restore and revive our souls when faint and withering under the influence of the atmosphere of evil around us. God forbid that we should make any other use of what we may term the Ziklag portion of David's history, save to apply it to our own hearts before God, and use it as a matter of solemn and soul-searching warning. For though it may be said that there is a wide difference between the standing and privileges of David, and those of the Church of God, now; yet, in every age and dispensation, nature is the same; and we seriously wrong our own souls if we fail to learn a wholesome lesson from the fall of one so high up in the school of Christ as David. Dispensations differ, no doubt, in their great leading features; but there is a wonderful analogy in God's principles of discipline, at all times, let the standing of His people differ as it may.

In following David, in his further sojourn, in the land of the Philistines, we only find fresh cause of humiliation. He obtains the grant of Ziklag, where he sojourns for sixteen months, during which period, though free from all fear with respect to Saul, he was at a distance from God and from Israel. It is, in one sense, a very easy matter to get out of a place of trial; but then we get out of a place of blessing also. It would have been much happier for David to remain in a position that left him exposed to Saul, while, at the same time, he enjoyed the protection of the God of Israel, than to seek safety from the arm of the king of Gath. However, when the pressure of trial is upon us, the thought of relief is sweet, and we are in danger of seeking relief in our own way. The enemy always has a by-road open to the man of faith. He had an Egypt for Abraham, and a Ziklag for David; and now he has the world, in all its varied forms, for us. "And truly, if they had been mindful of that country from whence they came out, they might have had opportunity to have returned." It is the opportunity to return that proves the genuine fixedness of purpose to go forward. The Lord leaves His people free, in order that they may "declare *plainly* that they seek a country." This is what glorifies God. It would avail nothing if we were to be compelled, as with bit and bridle, to go from earth to heaven; but when, through grace, we voluntarily abandon the things of earth, to seek those things which are above, this is to the glory of God, because it demonstrates that what He has to give is far more attractive than this present world. "*He led them forth* by the right way, that *they might go* to a city of habitation." (Psalm 107:7.) Grace not only leads forth from Egypt, but imparts the capacity and the desire to go to Canaan.

David, however, accepted of Ziklag, and instead of remaining as a homeless stranger in the Cave of Adullam, he becomes a citizen in the land of the Philistines. Nor does he now act the madman, as before: no, he now acts the part of a positive deceiver. He wages war on the Geshurites and Gezrites, and tells a lie about it, lest he should again lose his self-chosen place of protection. Yea, so far does he proceed in his unhappy course, that when Achish proposes to him to act as the ally of the Philistines, his answer is, "surely thou shalt know what thy servant can do. . . . And Achish said to David, Therefore will I make thee keeper of mine head forever. . . . Now the Philistines gathered together all their armies to Aphek: and the Israelites pitched by a fountain which is in Jezreel. And the lords of the Philistines passed on by hundreds, and by thousands: *but David and his men passed on in the rearward with Achish.*" (1 Samuel 28:2; 29:1-2). Here, then, we have a strange anomaly —a king of Israel about to be made keeper of the head of a Philistine, and about to draw the sword against the armies of the living God. Was ever anything like this? The slayer of Goliath, servant to a Philistine! Who could have looked for such a thing? Truly difficult is it for us to determine where all this would have ended, had David been left to push his plans to the uttermost; but this could not be. God was graciously watching His poor wanderer, and had rich and manifold mercies in store for him, as well as some humbling lessons and painful exercises of soul. The lords of the Philistines were the instruments made use of by the Lord to deliver David from his strange position.

They, judging from his past ways, could not be induced to trust him as an ally. "Is this not David? How can we confide in him?" A Philistine could never rely upon a Hebrew for cooperation against Hebrews. In a word, the men of this world can never place full confidence in one who has once decided for the truth of God; he is neither one thing nor the other. A saint who has got out of communion and gone back to the world, though he may go to the greatest lengths, will never be regarded or confided in as one of themselves; he will he suspected, just as David was by the Philistines. "Make this fellow return, that he may go again to his place which thou hast appointed him, and let him not go down with us to battle, lest in the battle he be an adversary to us" (1 Samuel 29:4-5). They would give him a certain place amongst them, but when it became a question of war between them and Israel, they would not acknowledge him; and they were wise, for let David *assume* what character he might, he could be *really* naught else save an enemy to the Philistines. He might *feign* himself to be mad; he might *pretend* to make war upon the south of Judah; but when matters came to a positive issue, David could only act consistently with his true character, as the slayer of ten thousands of Philistines. The fact is, from first to last, David was misunderstood; the Philistines did not know what it was that had sent him into their midst. There was far more in the apparent madman than they could fathom. They thought that he desired to be reconciled to his master, Saul, little imagining that they had before them one who was so soon to lay his hand upon the scepter of Israel, and to make them feel the weight of his power.

However, the Lord would not allow David to appear in the field against Israel. He sent him back, or rather He led him aside, in order that He might deal with him in secret about his course. "So David and his men rose up early to depart in the morning, to return into the land of the Philistines. . . . And it came to pass, when David and his men were come to Ziklag on the third day, that the Amalekites had invaded the south, and Ziklag, and smitten Ziklag, and burned it with fire; and had taken the women captives that were therein: they slew not any, either great or small, but carried them away, and went on their way" (1 Samuel 29:11-30:2) David is here made to feel the bitter result of his having gone to Achish for help in the day of his need. He had taken up his position amongst the uncircumcised, and must, therefore, be made partaker of their wretchedness. Had he remained amongst the mountains of Judah, he would have escaped all this sorrow; his God would have been a wall of fire round about him. But he had fled to Ziklag, to escape Saul, and then, as it were, at the very moment when Saul was falling on Mount Gilboa, David was weeping over the ruins of Ziklag. Surely it was not thus we should have expected to find David. "Then David, and the people that were with him lifted up their voice and wept, until they had no more power to weep. . . . And David was greatly distressed; for the people spake of stoning him" (vv. 4, 6). In all this God was dealing with His dear child, not to crush him, but to bring him to a right sense of the course he had been pursuing amongst the Philistines. Surely when David beheld the smoldering ashes of Ziklag, and felt himself deprived of his wives, he had a practical lesson as to the evil and sorrow of taking anything from the world. Perhaps we can hardly picture to ourselves a condition more truly heart-rending than that in which David found himself on his return to Ziklag. He had been, for a year and four months, pursuing a course that must have left him with an uneasy conscience toward God; he was cast off by those on whose protection he had thrown himself; his place of refuge was burned; his wives and property were gone; and lastly, his companions, those who had followed him in all his wanderings, were threatening to stone him.

Thus was David sunk to the very lowest ebb, in every point of view; all creature streams were dried up; and not only so, but the enemy might effectually ply his fiery darts at such a moment—conscience might work, and memory call up the scenes of the past: his abandoning the place of dependence; his flight to Achish; his change of behavior; his acting the madman; his telling a lie; his volunteering to fight against Israel, as the servant of the Philistines: all these things must have added to, in no small degree, his anguish of soul. But David was a man of faith after all, and notwithstanding all; he *knew the Lord,* and His "boundless stores of grace." This was his joy and comfort in this exceedingly dark moment of his career. Had he not been able to roll his heavy burden over upon infinite grace, he must have given up in utter despair. He had never before been so tested. He had met the lion and the bear in the wilderness; he had met the giant of Gath in the valley of Elah; but he had never met such an overwhelming array of circumstances before. Yet God was sufficient, and David knew this. Hence we read, *"David encouraged himself in the LORD his God."* happy, well-founded encouragement! Happy the soul that knows it! Happy he who could, in the twinkling of an eye, rise from the very deepest depths of human misery, up to God, and his never-failing resources! Faith knows God to be fully equal to all human need; human weakness; human failure; human sin. God is above all, beyond all, beneath all; and the heart that apprehends Him is lifted above all the trials and difficulties of the way.

There is no condition in which the Christian can find himself in which he may not count upon God. Is he crushed beneath the pressure of trial from external circumstances? Let him bring God's omnipotence, His resistless power, to bear upon these things. Is the heart oppressed by the burden of personal infirmity—truly a heavy burden? Let him draw upon the ex-

haustless springs of Divine compassion and mercy. Is the soul filled with horror, by the sense of sin and guilt? Let him have recourse to the boundless grace of God, and the infinitely precious blood of Christ. In a word, whatever be the burden, the trial, the sorrow, or the need, God is more than equal to all, and it is the province of faith to use Him. "David encouraged himself in the LORD his God" when everything around was dark and depressing. My reader, may we know the true blessedness of this. To have to do with God is real happiness and power. To disentangle our hearts from self and the things that surround us, and rise upward into the holy calmness of the Divine presence, imparts comfort and consolation beyond what one can utter. Satan's object is ever to hinder this. He would lead us to make present things, at all times, the boundary of our soul's horizon; he would seek to surround us with a thick, dark, impenetrable cloud, so that we might not recognize our Father's countenance, and our Father's hand, beyond it all.

But faith pierces the cloud, and gets upward to God; it looks not at the things that are seen, but at the things that are unseen: it endures, as seeing Him who is invisible; it can say to God,

> *"In darkest shades, if thou appear,*
> *My dawning is begun;*
> *Thou art my soul's bright morning star,*
> *And thou my rising sun."*

Truly David's return to Ziklag was a dark hour—one of his darkest; yet God appeared, and his dawning began. God appeared for his relief and restoration; He graciously removed the weight from his spirit; He burst the fetters, and let the prisoner go free. Such is the manner of God. He permits His children to taste the bitter fruit of their own ways, in order that they may return to Him, with full assurance that they can only be truly happy in His gracious and holy presence. Ziklag may shelter for a time, but it must speedily perish; and even while it lasts, must be purchased by the sacrifice of a good conscience toward God, and toward His people. A heavy price, surely, to pay for a temporary relief from pressure! How much better to endure the pressure for a time!

But, blessed be the name of our God, "all things work together for good." The death of the Philistine champion, and the sixteen months' sojourn in Ziklag; the cave of Adullam, and the house of Achish—all worked for David's good. The Lord makes the very failure of His children to yield them a rich harvest of blessing, inasmuch as it leads them to seek more prayerful vigilance of spirit, and a closer walk with Him. If our stumbles teach us to lean more implicitly upon God, we shall have to be thankful for them, however much we may have to be humbled at the remembrance of them. Humbling as David's Ziklag experience must have been to him, we may be sure he would not have been without it. It taught him more of the deep reality of God's grace and faithfulness; it enabled him to see, that when brought down to the very bottom of human things, he could find God there in all the fullness of His grace. This was a valuable lesson, and it will be our place to learn from it also. Are we able to lean on the Lord, amid the wreck and ruin around us? Is He beyond every one and everything to our souls? Can we encourage ourselves in Him, when all without and all within seems directly against us? Is His name dear to us, in this day of faithlessness, worldliness, and cold formality? Are we prepared to pursue the rest of our course through the desert in solitariness and desertion, if such should be needful? It may be, we have learnt to cease looking, in any way, to the children of this world; but are we prepared to lose the love

Lean on god

and confidence of our brethren? David's companions spoke of stoning him; yet the Lord was more precious to him than all; the Lord was "*his* God;" do we know the power and comfort of this? The Lord grant that we may know it more.)

Before closing this chapter, I would call the reader's attention to the instructive scene between David and the young man who was servant to the Amalekite. I do not, by any means, pretend to say that we are to regard it as a positive type; this would be saying too much; but we are certainly warranted in looking at it as a very striking illustration. An illustration of what? Let us see.

In order to appreciate the teaching of the Spirit in this Scripture (chapter 30:11-16) we must bear in mind the difference between Egypt and Amalek; the former is associated with Israel in the blessing of the latter day, "In that day shall Israel be the third with Egypt and with Assyria, even a blessing in the midst of the land: whom the LORD of hosts shall bless, saying, Blessed be Egypt my people, and Assyria the work of my hands, and Israel mine inheritance" (Isaiah 19:24-25). Amalek, on the contrary, is thus spoken of, "The LORD hath sworn that the LORD will have war with Amalek from generation to generation" (Exodus 17:16). An Egyptian, therefore, and an Amalekite stood in a very different relationship to Israel.

[Now this young man was an Egyptian, servant to an Amalekite, and his master left him because he had fallen sick. This was the treatment he had received from his Amalekite master; he had abandoned him in the hour of his need, because he was no longer able to be of service to him] But his very ruin and wretchedness threw him upon the sympathies of David, who refreshed him and revived his spirit. He found him faint and weak from the effects of his former service, and having restored his spirit, he inquired, "Canst thou bring me down to this company?" He here puts in his claim upon the service and devotedness of one who owed him everything under God; but the young man, though fully restored, was unable to act with David, until possessed of the full assurance of *life* and *liberty.* "Swear unto me by God," said he, "that thou wilt neither kill me, nor deliver me into the hands of my master, and I will bring thee down to this company." he could not serve David until he was fully assured of deliverance from the power of his old master.

All this is very striking as an illustration of the apostle's teaching in Romans 6. The believer needs to know his entire emancipation from the dominion of his old master, the flesh, before ever he can, with confidence, apply himself to the service of Christ. We have felt the bitterness of serving the flesh, as the apostle says, "What fruit had ye then in those things whereof ye are now ashamed? For the end of those things is death." It is quite impossible to walk in peace and liberty of heart until we know where death and resurrection have placed us. Until we know and believe that sin has no more dominion over us, we must, of necessity, be occupied about ourselves, for we shall be constantly discovering the working of indwelling corruption, and thus be filled with apprehension of being delivered over into the hands of our former oppressor. We may be very clear as to the theory of justification by faith; we may understand what it is to rest in the accomplished work of Christ in reference to sins that are past, and yet be so troubled about indwelling sin as to be quite hindered in our service to Christ and His Church. The gospel of the grace of God, when entered into in its divine fullness, sets the soul at rest, not only as to the past, but also the present and the future. The Lord forgives all our sins, and not only does He forgive sins, but also delivers from the power of sin, as we read in Romans 6, "Sin shall not have dominion over you: for ye are not under the law, but under grace." This is a truly precious truth for those who are daily harassed with the seeds of evil within. Though sin *dwells,* it shall not *reign.* And how is this deliverance accomplished? By death and resurrection. "He that has died is justified from sin." What claim has sin upon a dead man? None whatever. Well, then, God looks upon the believer as dead—dead with Christ, and risen again: and his power to deny the working of sin consists in his reckoning himself to be what God tells him he is. Thus, as David's oath set the young man's mind at rest, and enabled him to act with him against the Amalekites, so the word of Christ banishes fear and hesitation from the heart of the believer, and enables him, through the Spirit, to act against his former master—the flesh. Grace assures us that all our interests, for time and eternity, have been most fully provided for in the death and resurrection of Christ, and gives us to see that our only business now is to live to the praise of Him who died for us, and rose again.)

"Shall we continue in sin?" Could the young man, in this Scripture, have gone back again to his Amalekite master? Impossible. What fruit had he from his former service? Ruin and desertion. And what fruit had we? Death. The wages of sin is death. The world, the flesh, and the devil, can only lead us down to hell. Serve them how we may, death and destruction must be the end. Men may not see this; they may not wish to see it; yet it is not the less true. "It is appointed unto men once to die, but after this the judgment." This is the appointment; but Christ has borne all for the believer; death and judgment have passed away, and nothing remains but for the believer to accompany, in liberty and joy of heart, the true David against his enemies. Christ has done all for us that we might act for Him, in this the time of His rejection. He has suffered for us without the gate, and now calls upon us to go forth to Him, bearing His reproach. The believer does not act in order to get life, but because he has it. He starts on his

FULL ASSURANCE CONT

Christian career with the full assurance of pardon and acceptance in the Beloved. Perfect justification is his starting-post, and glory the goal. "Whom He justified, them He also glorified." It is well to be exceedingly simple in our apprehension of this great truth. Some imagine that we can never know that our sins are forgiven while here. Now, if we cannot know that our sins are forgiven, we cannot know that God's word is true, and Christ's work perfect. Will any one maintain this? If not, both rest on the same basis. The forgiveness of sins, and the truth of God's word, are linked together in the precious gospel of Christ. Doubt the forgiveness of sins, and you call in question the truth of Christ's words, "IT IS FINISHED," words uttered under the most solemn circumstances.

Yet we know how hard it is for the heart to repose with unquestioning simplicity on the truth of God, in reference to the perfect remission of sins, through the blood of Christ. Our thoughts are too shallow and contracted to take in all the effulgence of divine grace. We are too full of legalism, too full of self. We vainly think that we must add something to what Christ has done, whether that something be in the shape of works, feelings, or experiences. All this must be set aside. Christ *alone* is the great foundation, the eternal rock, the tower of salvation. To add even circumcision would be to make Christ of none effect, to fall from grace, and to make ourselves debtors to keep the whole law, and thus to expose ourselves to curse and wrath. "As many as are of the works of the law are under the curse."

May we cling to Christ, with a deeper sense of our own vileness and His perfectness. May we wrap ourselves up, as it were, in Him, while passing on through this cold and faithless world.

THE RETURN
OF THE ARK
2 SAMUEL 6 AND
1 CHRONICLES 8

We are now called to follow David from the scenes of his exile to those of his government. Saul has passed off the stage of history, having met death by the hand of an Amalekite; one of that very nation which he had disobediently spared. Solemn warning! Jonathan, too, had fallen in company with his father Saul, on Mount Gilboa, and David had given utterance to his sublime lament over both. David had ever carried himself towards Saul with the fullest sense of his being the Lord's anointed; nor did he manifest anything bordering upon a spirit of exultation when informed of his death; on the contrary, he wept over him, and called on others to do the same. Neither do we find anything like unbecoming haste to ascend the throne left vacant for him; he waited upon the Lord about it. "David inquired of the LORD, saying, Shall I go up into any of the cities of Judah? And the LORD said unto him,

Go up. And David said, Whither shall I go up? And he said, Unto Hebron" (2 Samuel 2:1) This was real dependence. Nature would have been eager to have rushed into the place of honor; but David waited on the Lord, and only moved as directed of Him. Happy would it have been for him had he continued thus to move on in child-like dependence.

But, alas! we have to trace far more of nature in David during the period of his elevation than during the period of his rejection A time of peace and prosperity tends to develop and bring to maturity many seeds of evil that might be nipped and blighted by the keen blast of adversity; David found the kingdom more thorny and dangerous than the wilderness.

David's first great error, after his accession to the throne of Israel, was in reference to the ark of the Lord. He desired to bring it up to the city of Jerusalem, and set it in its place. This was all right, and most desirable; the only question was, how was it to be done? Now, there were two ways of doing it. One prescribed by the written word of God and the other prescribed by the Philistine priests and diviners. The word of God was exceedingly plain and distinct in reference to this important matter. It pointed out a very simple and a very definite way of carrying the ark of the Lord of Hosts, even upon the shoulders of living men, who had been taken up and set aside for that purpose. (See Numbers chapters 3 and 8.) But the Philistines knew nothing of this, and, therefore, devised a way of their own, which, as might be expected, was directly opposed to God's way. Whenever men set about legislating in the things of God, they are sure to make the most fearful mistakes, because "the natural man receiveth not the things of the Spirit of God, neither can he know them, because they are spiritually discerned." And hence, though the plan adopted by the Philistines was very decent and orderly, as men would say, yet it was not of God. The ministers of the house of Dagon were poorly qualified to arrange the order of the divine service. They thought a wooden cart would do as well as anything else; it might have answered for the service of Dagon, and they knew no difference They had once trembled at the sight of the ark, but, through the unfaithfulness of Israel, it had lost its solemnity in their eyes, and though it had been most solemnly and impressively vindicated in their view by the destruction of their god, they understood not its deep significance, they knew not its wondrous contents; it was quite beyond them, and therefore they could devise nothing better than a mere lifeless ordinance for conveying it to its place.

But God's thoughts were not as theirs, and David ought to have known those thoughts, and acted upon them at the *1st* first; he should not have acted upon the thoughts and traditions of men in the service of God. He should have drawn his directions from a higher source, even from the book of the law. It is a terrible thing when the children of the kingdom form themselves after the model of the men of the world, and tread in their footsteps. They never can do so without serious damage to their own souls, and a great sacrifice of truth and testimony. The Philistines might construct a cart to carry the ark, and nothing whatever occur to show them the error of so doing, but God would not allow David so to act. And so now, the men of this world may put forth their canons, enact their laws, and decree their ceremonies in religion; but shall the children of God come down from their high position and privileges, as those who are guided by the Holy Spirit, and the blessed word of God, and suffer themselves to be guided and influenced by such things? They may do so, but they shall assuredly suffer loss.

David was made to learn his mistake by bitter experience, for "when they came unto the threshing floor of Chidon, Uzzah put forth his hand to hold the ark; for the oxen stumbled" (1

Chronicles 13:9). The wretched weakness, folly, and inconsistency of the whole thing was here fully displayed. The Levites, the ministers of God had borne the ark from Horeb to Jordan, and yet we have no record of any stumble. No; that was God's way; but the cart and oxen were man's way. This was the difference. Who would have thought that an Israelite would have deposited the ark of the God of Israel upon a wooden cart, to be drawn by oxen? Yet such is ever the sad effect of departing from the written word, to follow human traditions. "The oxen stumbled." What else could be expected? The arrangement was unquestionably "weak and beggarly," in the judgment of the Holy Spirit; and the Lord was only making this fully manifest. The ark should never have been in such a dishonoring position; oxen should never have been the bearers of such a burden.

"And the anger of the LORD was kindled against Uzzah, and he smote him, because he put his hand to the ark: and there he died before God" (1 Chronicles 13:10). Truly, "judgment must, begin at the house of God." The Lord judged David for doing what the Philistines had done without notice. The nearer a man is to God, the more solemnly and speedily will he be judged for any evil. This need not afford any encouragement to the worldling, for, as the apostle says, "If judgment first begin at us, what shall the end be of those that obey not the gospel of God? And if the righteous scarcely be saved, where shall the ungodly and the sinner appear?" If God judges His people, what shall become of the poor worldling? This is a startling inquiry. The Philistines, though they escaped the judgment of God in the matter of the cart, had to meet it in another way. God deals with all according to His own holy principles, and the breach upon Uzzah was designed to restore David to a right apprehension of the mind of God in reference to the ark of His presence. Yet it did not seem, at first, to produce the proper effect. "David was displeased because the LORD had made a breach upon Uzzah: wherefore that place is called Perez-Uzzah to this day. And David was afraid of God that day, saying, How shall I bring the ark of God home to me?" (2 Chronicles 13:10-12). There is much deep instruction in this. David was doing a right thing in a wrong way, and when God executed judgment upon his way of acting, he despaired of doing the thing at all. This is a very common error. We enter upon some right course of action in a wrong way, or in a wrong spirit, which God cannot own; and then our spirit, or method of action, is confounded with the service in which we were engaged. Now, we must ever distinguish between *what* men do, and *how* they do it. It was right for David to bring up the ark; it was wrong to put it on a new cart. The Lord approved the former, but disapproved and judged the latter. God will never suffer His children to persist in carrying on His work upon wrong principles. They may go on for a time with much apparent success, as "David and all Israel played before God with all their might, and with singing and with harps, and with psalteries, and with timbrels, and with cymbals, and with trumpets." This was very imposing. It would have been a difficult matter for any one to raise an objection to the cause of David in this proceeding. The king and all his captains were engaged in it; and the burst of music would have drowned any objection. But, how soon was all this exultation checked! "The oxen stumbled;" "Uzzah put forth his hand;" vainly imagining that God would suffer the ark of His presence to fall to the ground. He, who had maintained the dignity of that ark, even in the dark solitude of the house of Dagon, would surely preserve it from dishonor amid the mistakes and confusion of His people. It was a solemn thing to come near the ark of God —a solemn thing to approach that which was the special symbol of the Divine presence in the midst of His congregation.

It is a solemn thing to be the bearer of the name of Jesus, and the depositaries of the truth connected with His holy Person. We should all feel this solemnity more deeply than we do. We are too apt to regard it as a light thing to put our hand to the ark; but it is not, and all who attempt it will, like Uzzah, suffer for their error.

But, it may be asked, has anything been entrusted to the care and keeping of the, Church answering to the ark? Yes; the Person of the Son of God answers to the ark of old. His divine and human nature answers to the gold and shittim wood of the ark. The *materials* of the ark typified His *Person* as the God-man; while the *purposes* of the ark and mercy-seat typified His *work,* whether in life or in death. The ark enclosed the tables of testimony; and the Son of God could say, in connection with the body prepared of God for Him, "Thy law is within my heart." (See Psalm 40.) Again, the mercy-seat spoke of peace and pardon, of mercy rejoicing against judgement, to the poor sinner; and the apostle says, "He (Christ) is a mercy-seat for our sins." And again, "whom God hath set forth to be a mercy-seat."

Thus we perceive what a marked type the ark of the covenant was of Him who magnified the law and made it honorable—even Jesus the Son of God, whose glorious Person should be the special object of the saints' reverend and affectionate guardianship. And, just as Israel's moral power was ever connected with the right acknowledgment and preservation of the ark amongst them, so the Church's power will be found connected with her due maintenance of the doctrine—the great and all-important doctrine of the Son. It is in vain that we exult in the work of our hands, and boast ourselves in our knowledge, our testimony, our assemblies, our gifts, our ministry, our anything. If we are not maintaining the honor of the Son, we are really worthless—we are merely

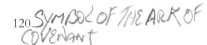
SYMBOL OF THE ARK OF COVENANT

walking in the sparks of our own kindling—sparks which shall speedily be extinguished, when the Lord is obliged, in very faithfulness, to come in and make a breach upon us. "David was displeased" at the breach. It was a grievous check to all the joy and gladness of the occasion; but it was needful. A faithful eye detected the wrong moral condition of soul that was betrayed by the wooden cart; and the breach upon Uzzah was designed as a corrective, and it proved an effectual one.

"David brought not the ark of God home to himself to the city of David, but carried it aside into the house of Obed-edom, the Gittite." This was David's loss; he forfeited much blessing and privilege by thus stopping short, for the ark of God could do naught but bless all who were rightly connected with it, though it was judgment to be connected with it other-wise, as in the case of the men of Beth-shemesh and Uzzah. It was a happy time for Obed-edom while the ark was in his house, for "the LORD blessed his house and all that he had." All the time that David was "*afraid*" and without the ark, Obed-edom was "*blessed*" with the ark. True, things might not just look so cheering; the blessing, instead of being diffused through the whole nation, as it would have been had all been right, was confined to the immediate circle of him who had the ark in his house. Still the blessing, though contracted, was as real and positive, as pure and truthful, as if the whole na-tion had been enjoying it. It could not be otherwise, inas-much as it was the result of the presence of the ark. God will ever be true to His own principles, and will ever make those happy who walk in obedience; and as He blessed Obed-edom during the three months that the ark was in his house, though even king David was "afraid," so will He now bless those who seek to meet in truth and simplicity, in the name of Jesus. "Where two or three are gathered together in my name, there am I." This is the great charter of our meeting. Where the presence of Christ is, there must be blessing. Weakness there may be, no doubt, and paucity, but still blessing and comfort, because Jesus is there; and the more we feel our own weakness, emptiness, and nothingness, the more will His presence be prized and loved.

Christians should seek to know more of the presence of Christ in their meetings. We do not lack sermons, nor power of eloquence, nor human intellect, nor anything that merely comes from man; we need the presence of Jesus; and without that all is cold, barren, and lifeless. But, who can tell the sweetness of realizing the presence of the Master? Who can give expression to the exquisite feeling known by those on whom the dew of the divine blessing drops? Blessed be God that any know it. Blessed be God that in this day, when the sad effects of human tradition are but too apparent in the Church, there is such a thing as the house of Obed-edom the Gittite, where the presence of the true ark, and the consequent blessing of God, can he known and enjoyed! Let us prize this more and more, amid the shadowy and unsatisfying forms and ceremonies that prevail around us.

We shall now dwell, for a little, upon God's gracious method of restoring the soul of His servant David. The life of faith is little more than a series of falls and restorations, errors and corrections; displaying, on the one hand, the sad weakness of man, and on the other, the grace and power of God. This is abundantly exemplified in David.

There is a considerable difference in the way in which the return of the ark is recorded in Samuel and in Chronicles; in the one we have the simple statement of the facts: in the other, we have the moral training through which the soul of David passed during the time that he was afraid of God, or, in other words, during the time that he was laboring under the effects of his own mistake. In Samuel we read, "And it was told king David, saying, The LORD hath blessed the house of Obed-edom, and all that pertaineth unto him, because of the ark of God. So David went and brought up the ark of God from the house of Obed-edom into the city of David with gladness." (2 Samuel 6:12.) David learnt that so far from standing aloof from the ark through fear, it was really his privilege and blessing to be near it. In 1 Chronicles 14:10-11, we find David in conflict with the Philistines, and obtaining victory over them. "David enquired of God, saying, Shall I go up against the Philistines? And wilt thou deliver them into mine hand? And the LORD said unto him, Go up; for I will deliver them into thine hand. So they came up to Baal-perazim; and David smote them there. Then David said, God hath broken in upon mine enemies by mine hand, like the breaking forth of waters; therefore they called the name of that place Baal-perazim (i.e. a place of breaches.)" There is a very great difference between "a breach" and "a place of breaches." God had made a breach upon Israel because of their error in reference to the ark: but as to the Philistines, it was not merely a breach made upon them, they were altogether in a place of breaches; and David might have learnt what a poor example he had followed when he made the cart to carry the ark. At least, he learnt his mistake, for in 1 Chronicles 15:1-2, we read, "And David made him houses in the city of David, and prepared a place for the ark of God, and pitched for it a tent. Then David said, None ought to carry the ark of God but the Levites; for them hath the LORD chosen to carry the ark of God, and to minister unto him for ever." And again, addressing the chief of the fathers of the Levites, he says, "Sanctify yourselves, both ye and your brethren, that ye may bring tip the ark of the LORD God of Israel unto the place that I have prepared for it. For because ye did it not at the first, the LORD made a breach upon us, for that we sought Him not *after the due order*} (1 Chronicles 15:12-13). Thus was David's soul fully restored. He was brought to see that to follow in the current of man's thoughts was contrary to "the due order." None can teach like God. When David was wrong, God made a breach upon him by his own hand. He would not allow the Philistines to do this: no; on the contrary, He allows David to see them in a place of breaches, and enables him to smite them—to break in upon them, like the breaking forth of waters. Thus God taught, and thus David learnt, what was "the due order," thus he learnt, as it were, to remove the ark from the new cart, and place it upon the shoulders of the Levites, whom the Lord had chosen to minister unto Him for ever. Thus he was taught to cast aside human traditions, and follow, in simplicity, the written word of God, in which there was not so much as a single word about a cart and oxen. "*None* ought to carry the ark of God but the Levites." This was very distinct. The entire mistake had arisen from forgetfulness of the word, and following the example of the uncircumcised, who had no capacity to understand the mind of God on any question, much less the solemn and important one of carrying the ark.

But in what a wonderfully gracious way did the Lord teach His servant! He taught him by victory over his enemies! Thus it is the Lord frequently leads His children into the apprehension of His mind, when they vainly seek to follow in the track of the men of this world. He shows them that they should not adopt such models. *The breach* taught David his mistake; *the place of breaches* taught him God's due order: by the former, he learnt the folly of the cart and oxen; by the latter, he learnt the value of the Levites, and the place that they held in the service of God. God must ever be true to His own principles; He would not allow His people to depart from His prescribed order with impunity. Hence, the ark would have remained to the end in the house of Obed-edom, had David not learnt to lay aside his own way of bringing it up, and adopt God's way.

"So the priests and the Levites sanctified themselves to bring up the ark of the LORD God of Israel. And the children of the Levites bare the ark *upon their shoulders,* with the staves thereon, as *Moses commanded, according to the word of the LORD*" (1 Chronicles 15:14-15). The Lord was glorified in all this, and He could therefore give real joy and gladness, strength and energy. There was no more stumbling of oxen; no more human effort to keep the ark from falling; the truth of God was dominant, and the power of God could act. There can be no real power where truth is at all sacrificed. There may be the appearance of it, the assumption of it, but no reality. How can there be? God is the source of power, but God cannot associate Himself with anything that is not in the fullest harmony with His truth. Hence, although "David and all Israel played before God with all their might," there was no appointment of Levites or singers according to the divine order. God was shut out by human arrangement, and all ended in confusion and sorrow. How different is it in chapter 15. There is real joy, real power. "It came to pass, when *God helped the Levites* that bare the ark of the covenant of the LORD, that they offered seven bullocks and seven rams. And David was clothed with a robe of fine linen, and all the Levites that bare the ark, and the singers, and Chenaniah the master of the song, with the singers" (1 Chronicles 15:26-27). In a word, this was a scene with which God could consistently connect himself: He did not help the oxen, He did not help Uzzah. Neither the oxen nor Uzzah had borne the ark, of old, through the waters of Jordan; neither had they borne it round the walls of Jericho. No; the Levites had carried it then, nor should any one, nor anything have been put in their place. God's order is, after all, the only happy one. It may not always commend itself to human judgment; yet it will ever have the stamp of Divine approval, and this is abundantly sufficient for every faithful heart. David was enabled to bear the sneer of contempt from Michal, the daughter of Saul, because HE WAS ACTING BEFORE THE LORD. Hear his fine reply to her reproach. "It was before the LORD, which chose me before thy father, and before all his house, to appoint me ruler over the people of the LORD, over Israel: *therefore will I play before the LORD. And I will yet be more vile than thus, and will be base in mine own sight.*" (2 Samuel 6:21-22). Precious determination! May it be ours, through grace. Base in our own eyes, happy in God. Humbled to the very dust in the sense of our own vileness, lifted up on high, in the sense of the grace and loving-kindness of our God.

The reader will remark that 1 Chronicles 16 is just the development of the spirit breathed in the above quotation. It is the hiding of self and the setting forth the character and ways of God. In short, it is a song of praise, which one has only to read to be refreshed thereby. I would only direct the reader's attention to the last verse, in which he will find the four great characteristics of the people of God fully set forth. "Save us, O God of our salvation, and gather us together, and deliver us from the heathen, that we may give thanks to thy holy name, and glory in thy praise." The Church of God is a saved company. *Salvation is the basis of everything. We cannot answer to any of the other characteristics in this copious verse, until we know ourselves as saved by the grace of God, through the death and resurrection of Christ.*

In the power of this salvation the Church is "gathered together," by the energy of the Holy Spirit sent down from heaven. The true effect of the Spirit's operation will be to lead into fellowship all who submit to His leading. His order is not isolation, but blessed *association*—association in the truth. But, if there be ignorance as to salvation, our gathering together will not be to the glory of God, but rather for the promotion of our own spiritual interests, as it is termed. Men frequently associate on religious grounds without the assurance of being fully and perfectly saved by the precious blood of Christ. This is not the Spirit's mode of gathering, for He gathers only to Jesus, and on the glorious ground of what He has accomplished. Confession to Christ, as the Son of the living God, is the rock on which the Church is built. It is not agreement in religious views that constitutes Church fellowship, but the possession of a common life, in union with the Head in heaven.

Now, the more this divine association is realized, the more will we enter into the next characteristic presented to us, viz., *Separation.* "Deliver us from among the Heathen." The Church is taken out of the world, though called to witness for Christ in it. All within the Church is under the government of the Holy Spirit; all outside, is under the lordship of Satan, the prince of this world. This is what Scripture teaches us about the Church. Hence, when the apostle speaks of excommunicating an offender, he says, "Deliver such an one to Satan." And again, "Whom I have delivered to Satan." Without the precincts of the Church is a wide and dreary domain, over which Satan rules, like that desolate region into which the leper was thrust from the camp of Israel. Finally, we have the Church presented as a *worshipping* people. "That we may give thanks to thy holy name." This follows from all that we have been looking at. Salvation, association, separation, and worship are all connected together. The Church, breathing the atmosphere of God's salvation, is led by the Spirit into holy and happy fellowship, and thus being separated unto Jesus, without the camp, presents the fruit of her lips to God, giving thanks to His name.

Seven

DAVID'S HOUSE AND THE HOUSE OF GOD

2 SAMUEL 7 AND 1 CHRONICLES 29

here is nothing in which the narrowness of the human heart is so manifested as in its apprehensions of divine grace. Legalism is that to which we are most prone, because it gives self a place, and makes it something. Now this is just the very thing that God will not allow. "No flesh shall glory in His presence," is a decree that can never be reversed. God must be all, do all, fill all, and give all.

When the Psalmist inquired, "What shall I render to the LORD for all His benefits?" it was, no doubt, a godly inquiry; but what was the reply? "*I will take* the cup of salvation." The way to "render" to God is to "take" yet more largely from His bounteous hand. To be a thankful, unquestioning recipient of grace, glorifies God far more than all we could render unto Him.

The gospel of the grace of God sets man entirely aside as

a ruined, helpless, guilty being; as one that, if left to himself, can do naught but spoil everything, and act in opposition to every scheme of blessing that could be devised on his behalf. Hence God must be the great Actor in redemption. By His gracious and all-wise counsels alone, it was planned before ever the mountains were brought forth. By His irresistible power alone it was accomplished in "the one offering of Jesus Christ once for all;" and by His eternal Spirit alone can any poor dead sinner be quickened into life, and made to believe the glorious and peace-giving tidings thereof.

Now, this stops man's mouth altogether, so far as his own righteousness is concerned. It excludes boasting, for man cannot boast in a sphere from which he is shut out in every character, save that of an unworthy recipient. How happy should all this make us! How happy is it to be the subjects of such grace that blots out all our sins, sets the conscience at rest, and sanctifies all the affections of the heart! Blessed forever be the fountain from which, and the channel through which, this saving grace flows to guilty, hell-deserving sinners!

The 7th chapter of 2 Samuel is full of instruction as to the great principle of grace: the Lord had done much for his servant David; He had raised him from the depth of obscurity to an exceedingly high elevation, and David felt this, and was disposed to look around him and survey the precious mercies which, in rich profusion, strewed his path. "And it came to pass, when the king sat in his house, and the LORD had given him rest round about from all his enemies, that the king said unto Nathan the prophet, See now, I dwell in an house of cedar, but the ark of God dwelleth within curtains." Observe, "David *sat in his house*." He was surrounded by his own circumstances, and thought it needful to do something for God; but again, he was in error as to his thoughts of building a house. The ark was within curtains, no doubt, because the time had not yet come for it to find a resting-place. God had ever moved in the fullest sympathy with his beloved people. When they were plunged in the furnace of Egyptian bondage, He was in a burning bush. When they were treading their long and dreary journey across the burning desert, His chariot traveled in company with them all the way, and He brought all His glory down into connection with the sand of the desert. When they stood beneath the frowning walls of Jericho, He was there as a man of war, with a sword drawn in His hand, to act in sympathy with them. Thus, at all times, God and His Israel were together: while they toiled, He toiled, and until they could rest, He would not rest. But David desired to build a house, and find a resting-place for God, while there were both "enemies and evil events." He desired to retire from the position and service of a man of war, and enter upon those of a man of rest. This could not be. It was contrary to the thoughts and counsels of the God of Israel. "It came to pass *that night,* that the word of the LORD came unto Nathan, saying, Go and tell my servant David, Thus saith the LORD, Shalt thou build me an house for me to dwell in? Whereas I have not dwelt in any house since the time that I brought up the children of Israel out of Egypt, even to this day, but have walked in a tent and in a tabernacle" (1 Samuel 7:4-6). The Lord would not allow another sun to rise without correcting the error of His servant; and His mode of correcting it was fully characteristic. He sets before him His own past actions toward Israel, and toward himself. He reminds him of how He had never sought a house or a rest for Himself, but had wandered up and down with His people, in all their wanderings, and been afflicted in all their afflictions. "In all the places wherein *I have walked* with all the children of Israel, spake I a word with any of the tribes of Israel whom I commanded to feed my people Israel, saving, Why build ye not me a house of cedar?" (v. 7). What lovely, what soul stirring grace breathes in these words! The blessed God came down to be a way-worn traveler with His travelling people. He would set His foot on the sand of the desert, because Israel was there; He caused His glory to dwell beneath a covering of badgers' skins, because His redeemed ones were in militant circumstances. Jehovah sought not an house of cedar; it was not for that He had come down to visit His people in the hour of their affliction in Egypt; He had come down *to give, not to take;* to spend and be spent, not to exact; to minister, not to be ministered to. True, when the people had put themselves under a covenant of works, at Mount Horeb, God had to test them by a ministration which was characterized by the words "*do*" and "*give;*" but, had they only walked in the power of God's original covenant with Abraham, they would never have heard such words uttered in connection with the terrific thunders of Mount Sinai.

When God came down to redeem them out of the hand of Pharaoh, and out of the house of bondage; when he bore them on eagles' wings, and brought them unto himself; when He made a way through the sea for his ransomed to pass over, and overwhelmed the hosts of Egypt in the depths; when he showered down manna from heaven, and caused the refreshing stream to gush from the flinty rock; when He took His place in the pillar of fire by night, and the pillar of cloud by day, to guide them through the trackless desert; when He did all these things for them, and many more, surely it was not on the ground of anything they could *give* or *do;* but simply on the ground of His own everlasting love, and the covenant of grace made with Abraham. Yes, this was the ground of His actions toward them; and, as for all they could do, it was only to reject His grace; trample on His laws; despise His warnings; refuse His mercies; stone His prophets; crucify His Son; resist His Spirit. Such were their actions,

132

from first to last; the bitter fruits of which they are now reaping, and shall reap, until they are brought, humbly and thankfully, to bow to His covenant of grace.

Now, it was by bringing all this in review before David that the Lord taught David his mistake in seeking to build a house. Shalt thou build me an house? whereas, . . . Now therefore so shalt thou say to my servant David, Thus saith the LORD of hosts, I took thee from the sheepcote [sheepfold] from following the sheep, to be ruler over my people, over Israel: and I was with thee whithersoever thou wentest, and have cut off thine enemies out of thy sight, and have made thee a great name, like unto the name of the great men that are in the earth. Moreover, I will appoint a place for my people Israel, and will plant them, that they may dwell in a place of their own, and move no more; neither shall the children of wickedness afflict them any more, as beforetime, and as since the time that I commanded judges to be over my people Israel, and have caused thee to rest from all thine enemies. Also the LORD telleth thee that He will make thee an house (2 Samuel 7:5, 8-12). David is here taught that his own history, like that of his people, was to be a history of grace from first to last. He is conducted, in thought, from the sheepfold to the throne, and from the throne into the boundless ages of the future, and sees the whole course marked by the actions of sovereign grace. Grace had taken him up; grace had set him on the throne; grace had subdued his enemies; grace was to bear him onward; grace was to build up his throne, and his house, to all generations. It was all grace. David might justly feel that the Lord had done much for him: the house of cedar was a great thing for the shepherd of Bethlehem; but what was it, when compared with the future? What was all that God had done, compared with what He would do? "When thy days be fulfilled, and thou shalt sleep with thy fathers, I will set up thy seed after thee, which shall proceed out of thy bowels, and I will establish his kingdom. He shall build an house for my name, and I will establish the throne of his kingdom forever." Thus we see, that it was not merely his own short span of forty years that was to be characterized by such actions of grace; no, his house was spoken of "for a great while to come," even forever.

Reader, to whom, think you, are we directed in all these wondrous promises made to David? Are we to regard them as fully actualized in the reign of Solomon? Surely not. Glorious as was the reign of that monarch; it by no means corresponded to the bright picture presented to David. It was, in one sense, but a passing moment, during which a bright gleam of sunshine flashed across Israel's horizon; for hardly are we conducted to the lofty pinnacle on which Solomon was elevated, when the chilling words fall on the ear, "*But, Solomon loved many strange women.*" Hardly has the cup of exquisite delight been raised to the lips, than it is dashed to the ground, and the disappointed heart cries out, "Vanity of vanities, all is vanity." "All is vanity and vexation of spirit."

The book of Ecclesiastes will tell us how far short the reign of Solomon came of actualizing the magnificent promises made to David in this 7th chapter of 2 Samuel. In that book we trace the yearnings of a heart that felt all aching void, and was ranging through creation's wide domain, in search of a satisfying object, but raged in vain. We must, therefore, look beyond the reign of Solomon to a greater than he, even to Him, of whom the Spirit in Zacharias speaks, in that fine prophecy in Luke 1, "Blessed be the Lord God of Israel; for He hath visited and redeemed His people, and hath raised up an horn of salvation for us in the house of His servant David; as He spake by the mouth of His holy prophets, which have been since the world began; that we should be saved from

our enemies, and from the hand of all that hate us; to perform the mercy promised to our fathers, and to remember His holy covenant, the oath which He sware to our father Abraham." Again, in the angel's address to Mary, "Behold, thou shalt conceive in thy womb, and bring forth a son, and shalt call His name Jesus. He shall be great, and shall be called the Son of the Highest; and the Lord God shall give unto Him the throne of His father David: and He shall reign over the house of Jacob forever; and of his kingdom there shall be no end." Here the heart can repose without a single check. There is no doubt, no hesitation, no interruption, and no exception. We feel that we have beneath our feet a solid rock, the Rock of Ages, and that we are not, like the writer of Ecclesiastes, constrained to lament the absence of an object capable of filling our hearts, and satisfying our desires; but rather, as some one has observed, like the bride in the Song of Solomon, to confess our entire lack of capacity to enjoy the glorious object presented to us, who is the "fairest among ten thousand, and altogether lovely."

"Of His kingdom there shall be no end." The foundations of His throne are laid in the deep recesses of eternity; the stamp of immortality is upon His scepter, and of incorruptibility upon His crown. There shall be no Jeroboam then, to seize upon ten parts of the kingdom; it shall be one undivided whole forever, beneath the peaceful sway of Him who is "meek and lowly of heart." Such are God's promises to the house of His servant David. Well might the astonished recipient of such mercies, when speaking of all that had been done for him, exclaim, "And this was yet a small thing in thy sight, O LORD God." What was the past, when compared with the future? *Grace* shone in the past, but *glory* glistened in the future. "The LORD will give grace and glory." Grace lays the foundation; glory garnishes the superstructure. This is true of all; it is true, in an eminent degree, of the Church, as we learn from the Epistle to the Ephesians: "Blessed be the God and Father of our Lord Jesus Christ, who hath blessed us with all spiritual blessings in the heavenlies with Christ; according as He hath chosen us in Him before the foundation of the world, that we should be holy and without blame before Him in love . . . to the praise of the glory of His *grace,* wherein He hath made us accepted in the beloved . . . that in the dispensation of the fullness of times . . . we should be to the praise of His glory" (Ephesians 1:3-4, 6, 10, 12). And again, "But God, who is rich in mercy, for his great love wherewith he loved us, even where we were dead in sins, hath quickened us together with Christ (by grace ye are saved;) and hath raised us up together, and made us sit together in the heavenly places in Christ Jesus: that in the ages to come he might shew the exceeding riches of his grace in his kindness toward us through Christ Jesus" (Ephesians 2:4-7).

Here we have grace and glory set forth most blessedly: grace securing, on immutable principles the full forgiveness of sins, through the precious blood of Christ, and full acceptance in His beloved Person; glory in the distance, gilding with its immortal beams the ages to come. Thus it is that the word of God addresses itself to two great principles in the soul of the believer; faith and hope. Faith reposes upon the past, hope anticipates the future; faith leans upon God's work already accomplished, hope looks forward with earnest desire, to His actions yet to be developed. This puts the Christian into a deeply interesting position; it shuts him up to God for everything. As to the past, he leans on the cross; as to the present he is sustained and comforted by the priesthood and promises; and as to the future, he "rejoices in hope of the glory of God."

But let us inquire, what was the effect produced upon David by all this burst of grace and glory on his spirit? One thing is certain, it effectually corrected his mistake in seeking, as another has said, to exchange the *sword* for the *trowel*. It made him really feel his own thorough littleness, and the greatness of God in His counsels and actions. "Then went king David in, and *sat* before the LORD, and he said, *Who am I, O LORD God?* It is impossible to convey, in human language, the deep experience of David's soul, as expressed in his attitude and inquiry on this occasion. First, as to his attitude, "*he sat.*" This gives us the idea of the most complete repose in God, without a single intervening cloud. There is no doubt, no suspicion, no hesitancy. God, as the mighty and gracious Actor, filled his soul's vision, and hence, to have entertained a doubt would be calling in question either God's willingness or ability to do all that He had said. How could he doubt? Impossible! The record of the past furnished too many substantial arguments in proof of both the will and ability of God to admit of a doubt on the subject.

And truly blessed is it thus to realize our place before the Lord—to allow the heart to dwell upon His wondrous ways of grace. To sit in his presence in the full, unclouded sense of His pardoning love. True, it is hard to understand why it should be so. Why He should set His love on creatures such as we. Yet, so it is; and we have only to believe and rejoice.

But observe his inquiry, "*Who am I?*" Here we have the hiding of self. David felt that he had nothing whatever to do in the matter. God was all, and self nothing, with king David, when he sat before the Lord. He no longer speaks of his actions, his house of cedar, his plan of building a house, etc. No; he meditates on the actions of God, and his own little doings sink into their proper nothingness, in his estimation. The Lord had said, "Shalt thou build me an house?" And again, "The LORD telleth thee, that He will make thee an house." In other words, the Lord taught David that He should be superior in everything, and that He could not, therefore, be anticipated in building a house. This might seem an easy lesson, but all who know anything of their own proud, self-righteous hearts, know that it was far otherwise. Abraham, David, Job, Paul, and Peter experienced the difficulty of hiding self and exalting God. This is, in fact, the most difficult lesson for a man to learn; for his whole being, naturally, is based upon the very opposite; the exaltation of self, and the setting aside of God.

It is needless to adduce any proofs of this; Scripture and experience alike demonstrate the fact that man seeks to be somewhat; and this cannot be attempted without setting aside the claims of God. Grace, however, reverses the matter, and makes man nothing, and God everything. "Is this the manner of man?" No, indeed, it is not the manner or law of man, but it is the manner of God. Man's manner is to set himself up, to rejoice in the works of his own hands, to walk in the sparks of his own kindling; God's manner, on the contrary, is to turn man away from himself; to teach him to look upon his own righteousness as filthy rags, to loathe and abhor himself; and relent in dust and ashes, and cling to Christ, as the ship-wrecked mariner clings to the rock. Thus was it with David, when he sat before the Lord, and losing sight of himself, allowed his soul to go out in holy adoration of God and His ways. This is true worship, and is the very reverse of human religiousness. The former is the acknowledgment of God, by the energy of faith; the latter is the setting up of man in the spirit of legalism. No doubt, David would have appeared to many a more devoted man, when seeking to build a house for the Lord, than when sitting in His presence. In the one case, he was trying to do something; in the other, he was apparently doing nothing. Like the two sisters at Bethany, of whom one would seem, in the judgment of nature, to have been doing till the work, and the other to have been sitting idle. How different are God's thoughts! David, sitting before the Lord, was in a right position; whereas David, seeking to build, was in a wrong one.

It must, however, be observed, that while grace leads us away from our own actions, it does not hinder real actions for God. Far otherwise, it only hinders unintelligent action. It does not abolish service, it only puts it in its right place. Hence, when David's soul was restored—when he learnt that he was not the man, nor his the time, to lay aside the sword, and take up the trowel, how readily did he acquiesce! How readily did he draw forth his sword from its scabbard, and take his place once more in the field of battle! How ready was he to be the militant servant to the end, and allow the curtain to drop upon him in that character! How ready was he to retire, and allow another to do the work!

In 2 Samuel chapter 8 we find David smiting, slaying, taking, and thus earning for himself a still more extensive fame as a man of war, and proving how effectually he had learnt the Lord's lesson. Thus will it ever be with all who learn the meaning of grace and glory. It matters little what the character of service may be, whether building the house or subduing the foes of the Lord; all is alike. The true servant is ready for anything. David came forth from amid the holy repose of the Lord's house to fight the Lord's battles, in order that, by his fighting, he might clear the ground for another to lay the foundation of that house, which his heart had so fondly desired to build. Truly this was the denial of self. David was the servant throughout. In the sheepfold, in the valley of Elah, in the house of Saul, on the throne of Israel, be maintained the character of a servant.

But we must pass to other scenes, in order to learn other and deeper principles in reference to David's connection with the house of God. He had to learn, in a remarkable manner, where the foundation of the Lord's house was to be laid. Let the reader turn to the 21st chapter of 1 Chronicles and read it. It is parallel with 2 Samuel 24, and furnishes the account of David's fall in numbering the people. He became proud of his hosts, or rather the Lord's hosts, which he would regard as his. He desired to count his resources, and he had to learn the emptiness thereof; the sword of the destroying angel mowed down seventy thousand of his boasted numbers, and brought home to his conscience, in terrible solemnity, his grievous sin in attempting to number the Lord's people. It, however, had the effect of eliciting much of the sweet, self-renouncing grace that was in David. Hear his touching words, as he exposes his own bosom to the stroke of judgment: "And David said unto God, Is it not I that commanded the people to be numbered? even I it is that have sinned and done evil indeed; but as for these sheep, what have they done? Let thine hand, I pray thee, O LORD my God, be on me, and on my father's house; but not on *thy* people, that they should he plagued." This was precious grace. He learnt to say, "thy people," and was ready to stand between them and the foe.

But there was mercy in the midst of wrath. By the threshing-floor of Ornan the Jebusite, the angel of judgment sheathed his sword. "Then the angel of the LORD commanded Gad to say to David, that David should go up, and set up an altar unto the LORD in the threshing-floor of Ornan the Jebusite." Here, then, was the spot where mercy triumphed, and caused her voice to be heard above the roar of judgment. Here the blood of the victim flowed, and here the foundation of the Lord's house was laid. "At that time, when David saw that the LORD had answered him in the threshing-floor of Ornan the Jebusite, then he sacrificed there. For the tabernacle of the LORD, which Moses made in the wilderness, and the altar of the burnt offering, were at that season in the high place at

Gibeon: but David could not go before it to inquire of God: for he was afraid, because of the sword of the angel of the LORD. Then David said, This is the house of the LORD God, and this is the altar of the burnt offering for Israel. And David commanded to gather together the strangers that were in the land of Israel: and he set masons to hew wrought stones to build the house of God" (1 Chronicles 21:28–22:2). Blessed discovery! By no other process could David have been so effectually, so impressively, so solemnly taught the place where the Lord's house should be built. Had the Lord pointed to Mount Moriah, and told David to fix upon a spot there to build the house, he never could have had such an idea of its deep significance. But why speak thus? The Lord knows how to lead His people, and to instruct them in the deep secrets of His mind. He taught His servant David by the instrumentality of judgment first, and mercy afterwards, and thus led him to the very spot where He would have His temple built. It was by his necessities he learnt about the temple to God, and he went forth to make preparation for it as one who had learnt God's character by his own thorough failure.

"This is the house of the LORD God." The place where mercy rejoiced against judgment—the place where the blood of the victim flowed–the place where David had his sin blotted out. This was very different from going to build on the ground of his dwelling in a house of cedar, as in 2 Samuel 7. Instead of saying, "Lo, I dwell in an house of cedar," he might say, "Lo, I am a poor, pardoned sinner." It is one thing to act on the ground of what *we* are; and quite another thing to act on the ground of what *God* is. The house of God must ever be the witness of His mercy, and this holds good whether we look at the temple of old or the Church now. Both show forth the triumph of mercy over judgment. At the cross we behold the stroke of justice falling upon a spotless victim, and then the Holy Ghost came down to gather men around the Person of Him who was raised from the dead. Just as David began to gather the hewed stones, and the materials for the joining of the house, the moment the place of the foundation was settled. The Church is the temple of the living God, of which Christ is the chief corner stone. The materials for this building were all provided, and the place of its foundation purchased, in the season of Christ's trouble; for David represents Christ in His sufferings, as Solomon represents Him in His glory. David was the man of war, Solomon the man of rest. David had to grapple with enemies; Solomon experienced rest from war. Thus do these two kings shadow forth Him who, by His cross and passion, made ample provision for the building of the temple which shall be manifested, in divine order and perfectness, in the day of His coming glory.

David proved, in the end, that though his *judgment* as to the time of building the house needed to be corrected, his *affection* for the house itself was no less fervent. He says, at the close, 'Now I have prepared with all my might for the house of my God the gold for things to be made of gold, and the silver for things of silver, and the brass for things of brass, the iron for things of iron, and wood for things of wood; onyx-stones, and stones to be set, glistening stones and of divers colors, and all manner of precious stones, and marble stones in abundance.' (1 Chronicles 29:2.) (In 2 Samuel 24:24, we read, in reference to the site on which the temple was built, "So David bought the threshing-floor and the oxen for *fifty shekels of silver.*' And in 1 Chronicles 21:25, we read, "So David gave to Ornan for the place *six hundred shekels of gold* by weight." The comparison of the two passages, so far from presenting any discrepancy, unfolds divine beauty. *Righteousness* valued the place at the former amount; whereas *grace* "gave" the latter. David had "set his affection to the house of his God," and therefore "gave over and above." This is very simple and *very* beautiful.) Thus does grace put service into its proper place, and not only so, but imparts an energy to it which ill-timed service can never exhibit. David had learnt lessons when he sat in the Lord's presence, and when he stood on the threshing-floor of Ornan the Jebusite, which wonderfully fitted him for making the needed preparations for the temple he could now say, "I have prepared with *all my might.*" And again, "Because I have set *my affection* to the house of my God, I have, of mine own proper good, of gold and silver, which I have given to the house of my God, *over and above* all that I have prepared for the holy house." His strength and affection were both devoted to a work that was to be brought to maturity by another.

Grace enables a man to hide himself and make God his object. When David's eye rested on the glittering pile that his devoted heart had raised, he was able to say, "Of *thine own* have we given thee." "Blessed be thou, LORD God of Israel our Father, for ever and ever. Thine, O LORD, is the greatness, and the power, and the glory, and the victory, and the majesty: for all that is in the heaven and in the earth is thine; thine is the kingdom, O LORD, and thou art exalted as head above all. Both riches and honor come of thee, and thou reignest over all; and in thine hand is power and might, and in thine hand it is to make great, and to give strength unto all. Now, therefore, our God, we thank thee, and praise thy glorious name. But *who am I,* and what is my people, that we should be able to offer so willingly after this sort? for *all things come of thee,* and of thine own have we given thee. For we are strangers before thee, and sojourners, as were all our fathers: our days on the earth are as a shadow, and there is none abiding. O LORD our God, all this store that we have prepared to build thee an house for thine holy name, cometh of thine hand, and is all thine own" (1 Chronicles 29:10-16). "Who am I?" What a question! David was nothing, and God was all and in all. If ever he had entertained the thought that he could offer anything to God, he entertained it no longer. It was all the Lord's, and He, in His grace, had allowed them to offer it all. Man can never make God his debtor, though he is ever seeking to do so. The 50th Psalm, the 1st of Isaiah, and the 17th of Acts, all prove that the unceasing effort of man, whether Jew or Gentile, is to give something to God; but it is a vain effort. The reply to man, thus endeavoring to make God his debtor, is, "If I were hungry, I would not tell thee." God must be the giver, man the receiver. "Who," says the apostle, "hath *first* given to Him?" The Lord will graciously take from those who are taught to say, "Of thine own have we given thee," but eternity will declare God to be THE GREAT FIRST GIVER. Blessed that it should be so! Blessed for the poor, guilty, broken-hearted sinner, to recognize in God the giver of all—of life, pardon, peace, holiness, everlasting glory! Happy was it for David, as he drew near the end of his checkered career, to hide both himself and his offerings behind the rich abundance of divine grace! Happy for him to know, as he handed the plan of the temple to Solomon, his son, that it should ever be the monument of God's triumphant mercy! The house was, in due time, to rise in magnificence and splendor from its foundation; the effulgence of the divine glory was yet to fill it from end to end; yet would it never be forgotten that it stood on that sacred spot where the devastating progress of judgment had been stayed by the hand of sovereign mercy, acting in connection with the blood of a spotless victim.

My reader, in passing from the temple of Solomon to that which in the latter day shall arise in the midst of God's beloved people, how fully may we trace the development of the same heavenly principles! Still more, when we pass from the earthly to the heavenly temple, may we behold the glorious triumph of mercy over every barrier; yea, rather, the glorious harmony effected between mercy and truth, righteousness and peace. From amid the brightness of millennial glory, shall Israel below, and the Church above, look backward to the cross as the place where justice sheathed its sword, and the hand of mercy began to erect that superstructure which shall shine, with everlasting light and glory, to the praise and honor of God, the blessed giver of all.

Eight

THE CONSPIRACY
2 SAMUEL 11

We are again called to follow David into the valley of humiliation—a deep valley indeed, where grievous sin and its bitter fruits are fully seen. It is really wonderful to trace the checkered path of this remarkable man. No sooner has the hand of love restored his soul, and set his feet again upon the rock, than he is again plunged into the depths of corruption. We have just seen his error in reference to the house of God graciously corrected, and we are now to behold him led captive in the chains of natural desire. Such, alas! is man—a poor, halting, stumbling creature, needing at every moment the fullest exercise of divine grace and forbearance.

The history of the most obscure believer will be found to exhibit, though on a smaller scale, all the roughnesses, inequalities, and inconsistencies observable in David's course. Indeed, it is this that renders the narrative of his life and times so peculiarly, so touchingly interesting to us.

Where is the heart unassailed by the power of unbelief, like David when he fled for refuge to the king of Gath? or by mistaken notions in reference to the Lord's service, like David when he sought to build a house for God, before the time? or by emotions of self-complacency and pride, like David when he sought to number the people? or by the vile lustings of nature, like David in the matter of Uriah the Hittite? If there be such a heart, it will find but little interest in tracing the ways of David. But well I know my reader has not such a heart, for wherever there is a human heart, there is also the susceptibility of all that I have been enumerating, and, therefore, the grace that could meet David mist be precious to every heart that knows its own plague.

The section of our history on which we are now entering is an extensive one, embracing many important principles of Christian experience and divine dealing. The facts of the case are, doubtless, familiar to all; but it will be profitable to look closely at them. David's sin led to Absalom's conspiracy. "And it came to pass, after the year was expired, at the time when kings go forth to battle, that David sent Joab, and his servants with him, and all Israel; and they destroyed the children of Ammon, and besieged Rabbah. *But David tarried still at Jerusalem*" (2 Samuel 11:1.) David, instead of being out at the head of his army, exercising himself in the hardships and fatigues of war, was quietly reposing at home. This was giving the enemy a manifest advantage over him. The moment a man absents himself from his post of duty, or retires from the place of conflict, he renders himself weak. He has taken off the harness, and will, undoubtedly, be pierced by the arrow of the enemy. While at work for the Lord, be the work what it may, nature is kept under pressure; but when at ease, nature begins to work, and feel the action and influence of external things. We should seriously ponder this. Satan will ever find mischief for idle hearts, as well as idle hands, David was made to feel this. Had he been at Rabbah, with his army, his eye would not have rested upon an object calculated to act upon the corrupt principle within, but the very act of tarrying at home afforded an opening for the enemy to come in upon him.

It is well to be ever on the watch, for we have a watchful enemy. "Be sober, be vigilant," says the apostle; "because your adversary, the devil, as a roaring lion, walketh about, seeking whom he may devour." Satan watches his opportunity, and when he finds a soul unoccupied with his proper service, he will surely seek to involve him in evil. It is, therefore, safe and healthful to be diligently engaged in service flowing out of communion with God, for we are thus in an attitude of positive hostility to the enemy; but if we are not acting in hostility, he will use us as instrument: for his own ends. When David failed in energy, as the captain of the hosts of Israel, he became the slave of lust. Sad picture! A solemn warning for our souls!

The believer is the subject either of the energy of the Spirit, or the energy of the flesh; if he fails in the former the latter will most assuredly predominate, and then he becomes an easy prey to the enemy. Thus it was with David. "At the time when kings go forth to battle," he was at rest in his house, and Satan presented a bait that proved too much for his poor heart. He fell—grievously, shamefully fell! Nor was his fall now a mere mistake. No; he fell into a deep pit of moral evil, of vile corruption, and his fall utters the solemn admonition, "*Keep under the body.*" Nature must be judged, or we shall make shipwreck.

And mark the fearful lengths to which David was carried in the commission of evil. Having sacrificed his character to indulge nature, he endeavors to make Uriah a cloak to screen him, from the public eye. His reputation must be maintained at all cost. He tries kindness, but in vain; he makes the wronged and dishonored Uriah drunk, but to no purpose; at last, he murders him by the sword of the children of Ammon. How dreadful! Did David really think that all was right when Uriah was out of the way? Did he forget that the eyes of the Lord were resting upon him in his evil course? It would seem that his conscience was not tender on this occasion, nor at all as susceptible of conviction as we should expect. Had it been so, he would assuredly have faltered and hesitated ere he added the sin of murder to that of adultery. He would have winced under the sharp reproof of Uriah—only the sharper because perfectly unintentional—when he said, "The ark, and Israel, and Judah, abide in tents; and my lord Joab, and the servants of my lord, are encamped in the open fields shall I then go into mine house?" etc. What a rebuke to David! The Lord and His people were in the open fields, conflicting with the uncircumcised foes of Israel, but David was at home enjoying the case and indulging the desires of nature. Surely, we may say, there was a time when David would not have been found reclining on his couch, when the hosts of the Lord were warring with the enemy. There was a time when he would not have exposed a faithful servant to the assault of the enemy, in order to save his own reputation. Such, however, is man; the best of men. When pride swells the heart, or lust dims the eye, who shall attempt to draw a limit to human depravity? Who shall define the fearful lengths to which even a David can go, when out of communion? Blessed forever be the God of all grace, who has ever proved Himself equal to all the demands of His wayward children! Who but God could deal with even one saint for a single stage of his history? When we remember His perfect estimate of the odiousness of sin, His perfect grace toward the sinner must fill the soul with adoring gratitude.

The Lord must maintain His holiness, however He may

deal with the sinner, and hence, in David's case, we find Him denouncing the most solemn judgment upon his house because of his sin. Nathan is sent to him in order to lead his conscience immediately into the presence of the holiness of God. This is the proper place for conscience to find itself. When not there, it will find various expedients, various subterfuges, and various cloaks. David said, when told of the success of his diabolical scheme in reference to Uriah, "Thus shalt thou say to Joab, Let not this thing displease thee, for the sword devoureth one as well as another." Thus did he think to hush up the whole matter. He vainly imagined that, when Uriah was out of the way, all would be well. But, there was an eye that could penetrate through all this covering that David's insensibility had cast over his heart and conscience. "The sword devoureth one as well as another," no doubt, and war has its vicissitudes; but this would not satisfy the holiness of God. No; the whole matter must be exposed; the dreadful meshes of evil in which Satan had entangled the feet of his victim must all be disentangled. The holiness of God's house must be maintained at all cost—His name and truth fully vindicated, and his servant scourged in the view of the whole congregation— yea "in the sight of the sun." It might seem, in man's judgment, to be wiser to hide from public view the chastisement of one who stood so high, but such is not God's mode; He will prove to every spectator that he has no fellowship with evil, by the judgment which He executes in the midst of His people. Nothing could avail to wipe off the stain that had been cast upon the truth of God but the public judgment of the transgressor. The men of the world may go on fix the present, and sin with a high hand; but those who stand in association with the name of the Lord, must keep themselves pure, or else be judged.

However, David would seem to have been most wonderfully insensible in this whole transaction. Even when Nathan's touching parable had set before him the blackness of his conduct, he, though roused to indignation at the selfish conduct of the rich man never took it to himself. "And David's anger was greatly kindled against the man; and he said to Nathan, As the LORD liveth, the man that hath done this thing shall surely die" (2 Samuel 12:5). Thus did he pronounce judgment upon himself unconsciously; he felt not his own sin as yet; perhaps he would have proceeded to find out and punish the offender, had not the prophet's word proved to be the very arrow of the Almighty to pierce his obtuse conscience. "*Thou art the man.*" Tremendous discovery! The sin was traced to its source and David stood his conscience-smitten, a broken hearted sinner in the presence of God. There is no more effort to screen himself, or maintain his reputation. "*I have sinned against the LORD,*" is the acknowledgment that flows truth from his wounded spirit. His soul was subdued by the power of the truth, and the 51st Psalm was his penitential utterance, as he lay prostrate in the dust, in the deep sense of his own personal vileness before the Lord. "Have mercy upon me, O God, according to thy loving-kindness according to the multitude of thy tender mercies blot out my transgressions." Here was David's well-known, oft-tried resource. He brings his heavy burden and lays it down beside the loving-kindness and tender mercy of God—the only place in which his harassed spirit could find repose. He felt his sin to be so heinous that nothing but the mercy of God could avail to blot it out. There, however, he found a "vast abyss" which could "swallow up" all his evil, and give him profound peace in the view of his own wretchedness.

Nor was it merely to be forgiven his sins that David desired; this he needed, no doubt, but he needed more he needed to be inwardly cleansed from the defiling power of sin itself. "*Wash me thoroughly* from mine iniquity, and cleanse me from

Sin Confess

my sin." The apostle says, "if we (i.e., believers) confess our sins, He is faithful and just (not merely) to forgive us our sins, (but also) to cleanse us from *all* unrighteousness." To be cleansed from unrighteousness is far higher than to be forgiven our sins, and David desired the latter its well as the former. Both are more difficult thing to confess our sin, than to ask for forgiveness. Really to confess before God the sin that we have committed, is a much more humbling thing than to ask for pardon in a general way. It is an easy thing to ask the Lord for pardon, but it is vain unless we confess our sins; and then, observe, it is a matter of simple faith to know that sins are forgiven us. The word is, "It we *confess* . . ."; David confessed his sin. "I acknowledge my transgressions; and my sin is ever before me. Against thee, thee only, have I sinned, and done this evil in thy sight; that thou mightest be justified when thou speakest, and be clear when then judgest." This was true conviction. There were no excuses, no laying blame on circumstances, no looking at individuals. It is simply *"I"* and *"Thee"* I a sinner, and Thou the God of truth. "Let God be true, and every man a liar." The secret of true restoration consists in taking our real place, as sinners, in the light of the truth of God. This is the apostle's teaching in Romans chapter 3. The truth of God is there set up as the great standard by which man's condition is to be tested. The effect of this is to bring the sinner down to the very depths of his own being, to the very bottom, as it were, of his moral and practical condition in the sight of God; it strips him of everything, and lays his inmost soul bare before a holiness which will not tolerate the least speck of sin in its presence. But when thus brought down into the dust of self-abasement and genuine confession, what do we find? We find God, in the solitariness and sovereignty of His grace, working out a perfect righteousness for the guilty and silenced sinner.

Here we find truth and grace presented to us in this most

important section of inspiration. Truth breaks the heart, grace binds it up; that stops the mouth, this opens it; stops it, that it may no longer boast of human merit; opens it, that it may show forth the praise and honor of the God of all grace.

David traveled, in spirit, through the truth afterwards set forth in Romans chapter 3. He, too, was led down into the profound depths of his nature. "Behold," he says, "I was shapen in iniquity, and in sin did my mother conceive me." Here he looks down to the very lowest point of depression. Man's original! What a thought! "*Shapen in sin.*" What good could ever flow from such a thing? Nothing! It is irrecoverable. And then observe the contrast: "Behold, thou desirest truth in the inward parts." God demands truth, and David had nothing wherewith to respond to his demand save a defiled original. What can fill up the vast chasm that exists between man born in sin, and God requiring truth in the inward parts? Nothing but the precious blood of Christ. "Purge me with hyssop, and I shall be clean: wash me, and I shall be whiter than snow." In other words, David throws himself, as a helpless sinner, into the arms of redeeming love. Happy resting-place! God alone can purge a sinner, and make him fit for His own presence. "Make me to hear joy and gladness; that the bones which thou hast broken may rejoice." God must do all; purge his conscience, open his ear again to the notes of joy and gladness, open his mouth to tell transgressors of His ways of love and mercy, create a clean heart within him, restore him the joy of His salvation, uphold him by his free Spirit, deliver him from blood-guiltiness. In short, from the moment that Nathan's word fell with divine power upon David's heart, he cast the crushing weight of his burden upon infinite grace, exercised through the precious blood of atonement, and thus, so far as he was personally concerned, he could rejoice in a perfect settlement of the question which his sin had raised between his conscience and

God. Grace gained a glorious triumph and David retired from
the field, scared, indeed, and sorely wounded, yet with a deep-
ened experience of who God was, and what grace had done
for his soul.

Still, David's sin produced its own bitter fruits in due time.
This must ever be so. Nothing can interfere with the realization
of that solemn word of the apostle, "Whatsoever a man soweth,
that shall he also reap." Grace may pardon the individual, but
the results of sin will assuredly appear, even though the sinner
may enjoy the deepest and sweetest experiences of divine love
and restoring grace, while actually under the rod. We shall see
this abundantly exemplified in David. He was, as we know, fully,
blessedly, divinely pardoned, washed, and accepted; nevertheless, he had to hearken to the solemn denunciation, "Now,
therefore, the sword shall never depart from thine house; because thou hast despised me, and hast taken the wife of Uriah
the Hittite to be thy wife." Observe, "thou hast despised ME."
David had sought to hide his sin from public view by putting
Uriah out of the way, forgetting the all-seeing eye of Jehovah,
and forgetting, too, the honor of His *holy* name. Had he remembered the Lord, at the moment when nature was causing
her voice to be heard within, he would not have fallen into the
snare. The sense of God's presence is the great preservative
from evil; but how often are we more influenced by the presence of our fellow-man, than we are by the presence of God.
"I have set the LORD always before me; because He is on my
right hand, I shall not be moved." If we fail to realize God's
presence as a preservative *against* evil, we shall be made to feel
it as a judgment *because of* it.

"The sword shall never depart from thine house." Contrast
this with the glorious promises made to David in chapter 7, and
yet it is the same voice that falls on the ear in the denunciation
and in the promise, though in a tone so awfully different; in

the latter, grace; in the former, holiness is heard. "Because by this deed thou hast given great occasion to the enemies of the LORD to blaspheme, the child that is born unto thee shall surely die." The death of the child, however, was but the first sound of the tornado of judgment that was about to burst upon David's house. He might fast, pray, humble himself, and lie prostrate in the dust, but the child must die; judgment must take its course, the consuming fire burn up every particle of the material submitted to its action. The sword of man "devours one as well as another;" but the sword of God falls on the head of the offender. Things must work and come to a head; the stream may flow, for a long time, under ground, but sooner or later it will burst forth. We may go on for years in a course of secret evil, in the cultivation of some unholy principle, in the indulgence of some unholy lust, in the gratification of some unholy temper or feeling, but the smoldering flame must ultimately break forth, and show us the real character of our actions. This is a truly solemnizing reflection. We cannot hide things from God, nor cause Him to think that our wrong ways are all right. We may try to reason ourselves into such a thought; we may persuade our hearts by very plausible arguments that such and such things are right, and good, and lawful; but "God is not mocked: whatsoever a man soweth, that shall he also reap."

Yet what grace shines out in this, as in every scene of David's remarkable career. Bathsheba becomes the mother of Solomon, who occupied the throne of Israel during the most glorious period of their history, and who also stands in that privileged line through which, according to the flesh, Christ came! This is truly divine! It is altogether worthy of God. The darkest scene in David's life becomes, under the hand of God, the means of richest blessings. Thus did the eater yield meat, and the strong sweetness. We know how this principle characterizes all the ways of God with his people. He judges their evil, no doubt, but pardons their sin, and makes their very failures the channel through which grace flows to them. Blessed, forever, be the God of all grace, who pardons our sins, restores our souls, bears with our many infirmities, and causes us to triumph, even through weakness.

How must David have felt ever after, as his eye rested upon his Solomon, "*the man of rest,*" his Jedidiah, "*the beloved of the Lord!*" He would remember his own humiliating fall; he would remember God's adorable grace. And, my beloved Christian reader, is it not just thus with ourselves? What is our history day by day, but a history of falls and restorations, of ups and downs? Nothing more; and thank God for the assurance that "grace all the work shall crown, through everlasting days."

At the close of this 12th chapter of 2nd Samuel, we find David again in conflict with the enemy, his proper place. "And David gathered all the people together, and went to Rabbah, and fought against it and took it. . . . And he brought forth the people that were therein, and put them under saws, and under harrows of iron, and under axes of iron, and made them pass through the brick-kiln; and thus did he to all the cities of the children of Ammon. So David and all the people returned to Jerusalem."

And now begins the heavy tale of David's woes, the fulfillment of the prophet's denunciation that the sword should never depart from his house. Chapter 13 records two of the most diabolical acts that ever stained a family circle. Amnon, the son of David, offers dishonor to the sister of Absalom, and Absalom murders Amnon and then flees to Geshur, where he remains three years. David allows him to return, contrary to the positive command of the law. Even had he been but a man-slayer, he should have remained in a city of refuge; but he was a murderer, and, with his murder upon him, he is received back again upon natural grounds—no confession, no judgment, no judgment, no atonement. "The king kissed Absalom." Yes, the king kissed the murderer, instead of allowing the law of the God of Israel to take its course. What then? "It came to pass after this, that Absalom prepared chariots and horses, and fifty men to run before him." This was the next step. David's inordinate tenderness only paved the way for Absalom's open rebellion. Terrible warning! Deal tenderly with evil, and it will, assuredly, rise to a head, and crush you in the end. On the other hand, meet evil with a face of flint, and your victory is sure. Sport not with the serpent, but at once crush it beneath your foot. Plain, unflinching decision is, after all, the safest and happiest path. It may be trying at first, but the end is peaceful.

But observe how Absalom works. He begins by creating a want in the hearts of the men of Israel. "And Absalom rose up early, and stood beside the way of the gate: and it was so, that when any man that had a controversy came to the king for judgment, then Absalom called unto him, and said, Of what, city art thou? . . . See thy matters are good and right; but *there is no man, deputed of the king to hear thee.* Absalom said, moreover, Oh, that I were made judge in the land, that every man which hath an suit or cause might come unto me, and I would do him justice. And it was so that when any man came nigh to him to do him obeisance, he put forth his hand, and took him and kissed him. . . . So Absalom stole the hearts of the men of Israel" (2 Samuel 15:2–6). The enemy's way is first to create a want, to produce a blank, and then proceed to fill it up with something, or some one, of his own providing. Those whose hearts were fully satisfied with David had no room for Absalom.

This is a fine principle when applied to our hearts in reference to Christ. If we are filled with Him we have no room for anything beside. It is only when Satan succeeds in creating a

want in our hearts that he introduces something of his own.
When we are able in truth to say, "The Lord is my portion," we
are safe from the influence of Satan's attractive baits. The Lord
keep us in the happy and holy enjoyment of Himself; that so
we may he able to say with one of old, "I try to lay up all my
good things in Christ, and then a little of the creature goes a
great way."

However, Absalom stole the hearts of the men of Israel.
He came in by flatteries, and usurped David's place in their
hearts and affections. He was a comely person, well adapted
to captivate the multitude. "In all Israel there was none to be
so much praised as Absalom for his beauty: from the sole of
his foot even to the crown of his head there was no blemish
in him." But his beauty and his flattery had no effect upon
those who were near the person of David. When the messenger
came, saying, "The hearts of the men of Israel are after Absalom," it became manifest who was for David. "And David said
unto all his servants that were with him at Jerusalem, Arise,
and let us flee. . . . And the king's servants said unto the king,
Behold, thy servants are ready to do whatsoever my lord the
king shall appoint.. . . . And the king went forth, and all the
people after him, and tarried in a place that was far off. And all
his servants passed on *beside him,* and all the Cherethites, and
all the Pelethites, and all the Gittites, six hundred men which
came after him from Gath, passed on before the king. . . . And all
the country wept with a loud voice, and all the people passed
over; the king also himself passed over the brook Kidron, and
all the people passed over, toward the way of the wilderness"
(2 Samuel 15:14-23). Thus were there many hearts who loved
David too well to be drawn away by the ensnaring influence
of Absalom. Those who had been with David in the days of his
exile were near his beloved person in this day of his deep sorrow. "And David went up by the ascent of Mount Olivet, and

wept as he went up, and had his head covered; and he went barefoot; and all the people that were with him covered every man his head, and they went up, weeping as they went up." This is a deeply touching and interesting scene. In fact, David's grace shines out more during this conspiracy than at any period of his life. And not only does David's grace appear in a striking point of view, but the genuine devotedness of his dear people also. When we behold a loving band of followers thronging round the weeping, the barefooted David, our hearts are far more deeply touched than when we see them thronging round his throne. We are more thoroughly convinced that his *person,* and not his office, was the center of attraction. David had nothing to offer his followers now save fellowship in his rejection; yet was there a charm about him, to those who knew his person, that bound them to him at all times. They could weep with him; as well as conquer with him. Hear the language of a genuine lover of David "And Ittai answered the king, and said, As the LORD liveth, and as my lord the king liveth, surely in what place my lord the king shall be, whether in death or life, even there also will thy servant be." Life or death; it was all alike, in companionship with David.

However, in looking through these chapters, there is nothing that so strikes us as David's beautiful subjection of spirit. When Zadok would bring the ark in his weeping train, he says, "Carry back the ark of God into the city; if I shall find favor in the eyes of the LORD, He will bring me again, and show me both it, and His habitation; but if He thus say, I have no delight in thee, behold, here am I, let Him do to me as seemeth good unto Him" (2 Samuel 15:25).

When the insulting Benjamite, Shimei, came forth to curse and cast stones at him, and Abishai desired permission to take off his head, his answer is, "What have I to do with you, ye sons of Zeruiah? So let him curse, because the LORD hath said unto him, Curse David. Who shall then say, Wherefore hast thou done so?" In short, he meekly bows his head to the dealings of God. He felt, no doubt, that he was only reaping the fruit of his sin, and he accepted it. He saw God in every circumstance, and owned Him with a subdued and reverent spirit. To him it was not Shimei, but the Lord. Abishai saw only the man, and desired to deal with him accordingly. Like Peter afterwards, when he sought to defend his beloved Master front the band of murderers sent to arrest Him. Both Peter and Abishai were living upon the surface, and looking at secondary causes. The Lord Jesus was living in the most profound subjection to the Father. "The cup which my Father hath given me, shall I not drink it?" This gave Him power over everything. He looked beyond the instrument to God beyond the cup to the hand that had filled it. It mattered not whether it were Judas, Herod, Caiaphas, or Pilate; He could say, in all, "*My Father's cup*".

Thus, too, was David, in his measure, lifted above subordinate agents. He looked right up to God, and with unshod feet, and covered head, he bowed before Him. "The LORD hath said unto him, Curse David." This was enough.

Now, there are, perhaps, few things in which we so much fail as in apprehending the presence of God, and his dealing with our souls in every circumstance of daily life. We are constantly ensnared by looking at secondary causes; we do not realize *God in everything.* Hence Satan gets the victory over us. Were we more alive to the fact that there is not an event which happens to us, from morning to night, in which the voice of God may not be heard, the hand of God seen, with what a holy atmosphere would it surround us! Men and things would then be received as so many agents and instruments in our Father's hand; so many ingredients in our Father's cup. Thus would our minds be solemnized, our spirits calmed, our hearts subdued. Then we shall not say, with Abishai, "Why should this dead dog curse my lord the king? let me go over, I pray thee, and take off his head." Nor shall we, with Peter, draw the sword of natural excitement! How far below their respective masters were both these affectionate though mistaken men! How must the sound of Peter's sword have grated on his Master's ear, and offended His spirit! And how must Abishai's words have wounded the meek and submitting David! Could David defend himself while God was dealing with his soul in a manner so solemn and impressive? Surely not. He dare not take himself out of the hands of the Lord. He was His for life or death—as a king or an exile. Blessed subjection!

But, as has been already remarked, the record of this conspiracy not only exhibits David's subjection to God, but also the devotedness of David's friends to his person, whether mistaken or otherwise. His mighty men are seen thronging round him on his right hand and his left, and sharing with him the insults and execrations of Shimei. They had been with him in the hold, with him on the throne, with him in the field, and they are now with him in his humiliation.

Shobi and Barzillai come forth to minister to him and his men with princely liberality. In short, the thoughts of many hearts were revealed in the season of David's sorrow. It was manifest who loved David for his own sake; and, no doubt, he returned to his house and his throne with a fuller and deeper confidence in the genuine affection of those around him.

There is, however, one character introduced to our notice, upon which we must dwell for a little. I allude to Mephibosheth, the son of Jonathan. Hardly had David taken his seat on the throne, when he gave utterance to those memorably gracious words, "Is there yet any that is left of *the house of Saul,* that I may show *the kindness of God* unto him?" "The house of Saul!" "The kindness of God!" What words! Saul had been his most implacable enemy; yet, being now on the throne, the brilliancy of his position, and the fullness of Divine grace, enabled him to sink in oblivion the acts of the past, and to manifest, not merely the kindness of David, but the kindness of God.

10 Now, the kindness of God is marked by this special characteristic, that it is exercised toward His enemies. "If, while we were enemies, we were reconciled to God by the death of His Son. . . ." Such was the kindness that David desired to show to a member of the house of Saul. "Now, when Mephibosheth, the son of Jonathan, the son of Saul, was come unto David, he fell on his face, and did reverence. . . . And David said unto him, Fear not, for I will surely show thee kindness, . . . and thou shalt eat bread at my table continually. And he bowed himself, and said, What is thy servant, that thou shouldest look on such a dead dog as I am?" Here, then, is a lovely specimen of the kindness of God, and here, too, we are presented with the ground of Mephibosheth's devotedness to David. Though having no more claim upon him than an enemy, or a dead dog, yet is he taken up in grace, and set down at the king's table.

But Mephibosheth had a faithless servant, who, to promote his own ends, misrepresented him to the king. The opening verses of chapter 16 will furnish the reader with an account 3,4 of Ziba's actions. He pretends kindness to David, and blackens the character of Mephibosheth, in order to get possession of his land. He takes advantage of his master's weakness of body, deceives and maligns him. What a picture!

The truth, however, came to light, and the wronged one was fully vindicated. On David's return, when all the trouble 19:24-30 was over, and Absalom perished from the scene, "Mephibosheth, the son of Saul, came down to meet the king, and had neither dressed his feet, nor trimmed his beard, nor washed his clothes, from the day the king departed until he came again in peace. Such is the Spirit's testimony to this interesting character. The absence of his beloved master deprived him of every motive to adorn his person. While David was away, Mephibosheth was a mourner. A true picture of what the saint ought to be now, during the period of his Master's absence. Fellowship with an absent Lord should impart a tone of thorough separation to the Christian character. The question is not at all what a Christian may, or may not do. No, an affectionate heart will suggest the true course to be adopted by all those who are looking for the king's return. What a truly divine spring of action does the absence of Jesus furnish! "If ye then be risen with Christ, seek those things which are above." Ask the spiritual man, why does he abstain from things that he might enjoy? His answer is, *Jesus is absent.* This is the highest motive. We do not want the rules of a cold and barren formalism to regulate our ways; but we want a more fervent affection for the Person of Christ, and a more lively desire for His speedy return. We, like Mephibosheth have experienced the kindness of God—precious kindness! We have been taken up from the depths of our ruin, and set among the princes of God's people. Should we not, therefore, love our Master? Should we not desire to see His face? Should we not regulate our present conduct by constant reference to Him? Would that our hearts were able to yield a ready answer in the affirmative. But, alas! here we fail. We are little like Mephibosheth; we are but too well disposed to pamper, decorate, and minister to our odious nature. Too ready to walk in the unchecked enjoyment of the things of this life; its riches, its honors, its comforts, its refinements, its elegancies, and the more so because we imagine we can do all these things without forfeiting our title to the name and privileges of Christians. Vain, detestable selfishness! Selfishness, which shall be put to the blush in the day of Christ's appearing.

Had Ziba's account of Mephibosheth been true, how could the latter have replied to David when he said, "Wherefore wentest thou not with me, Mephibosheth?" But he was able to answer, "My lord, O king, my servant deceived me: for thy servant said, I will saddle me an ass, that I may ride thereon, and go to the king; because thy servant is lame. And he hath slandered thy servant unto my lord the king; but my lord the king is as an angel of God; do, therefore, what is good in thine eyes. For all of my father's house were but dead men before my lord the king; yet didst thou set thy servant among them that did eat at thine own table. What right, therefore, have I yet to cry any more unto the king?" (2 Samuel 19:26-28). Here was simple integrity of heart. Unaffected devotedness must develop itself. The contrast between Ziba and Mephibosheth is truly striking. The former was seeking for the inheritance; the latter only desired to be near the king. Hence, when David said, "Why speakest thou any more of thy matters? I have said, thou and Ziba divide the land," Mephibosheth at once proved the direction in which his thoughts and desires were flowing; "Yea," said he, "*let him take all,* forasmuch as my lord the king is come again in peace unto his own house." His heart was engaged about David, not about the "matters." How could he stand on a footing with Ziba? How could he divide the land with such an one? Impossible! The king had returned; this was enough for him. To be near to him was better than all the inheritance of the house of Saul. "Let him take *all.*" Nearness to the person of the king so filled, so satisfied the heart of Mephibosheth, that he could, without any difficulty, give up all that for which Ziba had so diligently acted the deceiver and the slanderer.

Just so will it be with those who love the name and Person of the Son of God. The prospect of His loved appearing will deaden their affections for the things of this world. With them it will not be a question of lawfulness or unlawfulness: such terms are far too cold for an affectionate heart. The very fact of their looking out for the morning, will, of necessity, turn their hearts away from all beside; just as gazing intently at any special object necessarily turns one away from everything else. If Christians realized more of the power of the blessed hope, how would they walk above and apart from the world? The enemy is well aware of this, and hence he has labored hard to reduce this hope to the level of a mere speculation—a peculiar tenet, possessing little or no practical power, no solid or indisputable basis. That section of inspiration, too, which specially unfolds the events connected with thin coming of Christ, he has succeeded in involving in almost total neglect. The book of Revelation has, until very recently, been regarded as a book of such profound and inextricable mystery, that few, if any, could approach it. And even since the attention of Christians has been more particularly directed to its study, he has introduced and built up such conflicting systems; has set forward such jarring interpretations, that simple minds are well-nigh scared away from a subject which seems, in their judgment, to be inseparably connected with mysticism and confusion.

Now there is just one grand remedy for all this evil; *a genuine love of the appearing of Jesus.* Those who are waiting for that will not dispute much about the mode of it. Indeed, we may set it down as a fixed principle, that in proportion as affection becomes dead, will the spirit of controversy prevail.

All this is very simply and very strikingly illustrated in the narrative of Mephibosheth. He felt that he owed everything to David; that he had been saved from ruin, and raised to dignity. Hence, when David's place was occupied by a usurper, Mephibosheth's whole appearance and manner proved that he had no sympathy with the existing state of things; he was estranged from it all, and only sighed for the return of him whose

kindness had made him all he was. His interests, his destinies, his hopes, were all bound up with David, and nothing but, his return could make him happy.

Oh! that it were thus with us, my beloved Christian reader. Would that we really entered more into our true character, as strangers and pilgrims, in the midst of a scene where Satan rules. The time is coming when our beloved King shall be brought back, amid the affectionate acclamations of His people, when the usurper shall be hurled from his throne, and every enemy crushed beneath the footstool of our glorious Immanuel. The Absaloms, the Ahithophels, the Shimeis, shall find their proper place; and, on the other hand, all who, like Mephibosheth, have mourned the absent David, shall have all the desires of their longing hearts abundantly satisfied. "How long, O Lord?" May this be our cry, as we eagerly look for the earliest sound of His chariot wheels. The way is long, rough, and painful; the night dark and depressing; but the word is, "Be patient, brethren." "He that shall come will come, and will not tarry. Now the just shall live by faith; but if any man draw back, my soul shall have no pleasure in him."

Into the further details of Absalom's conspiracy, I do not now mean to enter. He met the end his deeds merited, though a father's heart might grieve and a father's tears flow for him. Moreover, his history may justly be viewed as a type of that great prophetic character, who, as Daniel informs us, "shall obtain the kingdom by flatteries." This, however, and many other points full of interest, I shall leave the reader to deduce from the sacred text for himself, praying the Lord to make the study of His own word refreshing and edifying, in this day of darkness and confusion. Never was there a time when Christians needed more to give themselves to the prayerful study of Scripture. Conflicting opinions and judgments, strange notions and baseless theories are abroad, and the simple mind knows not whither to turn. Blessed be God, His word is before us in all its lucid simplicity, and in it we have the eternal fountain of truth, the immutable standard by which everything must be judged; all therefore, that we need is a mind fully subject to its teaching. "If thine eye be single, thy whole body shall be full of light."

Nine

THE SONG AND
LAST WORDS
2 SAMUEL 22
AND PSALM 18

he 22nd chapter of 2 Samuel contains David's magnificent song, and is parallel with Psalm 18. It is the utterance
of the spirit of Christ in David connected with His triumph
over death, through the mighty energy of the power of God
(Ephesians 1:19). In it, as the inspired heading teaches us, David
presents his praise to God for deliverance from the hand of all
his enemies, and the hand of Saul particularly He thankfully
recounts the glorious actions of God on his behalf, yet in such
language as at once leads us from David and all his conflicts, to
that terrible conflict which raged around the grave of Jesus,
when all the powers of darkness were ranged, in fierce array
against God. Tremendous was the scene! Never before, and
never since, was such a battle fought or such a victory gained,
whether we look at the contending powers, or the consequences resulting Heaven, on the one side, and hell on the

other. Such were the contending powers. And as to the consequences resulting, who shall recount them? The glory of God and of His Christ, in the first place the salvation of the Church; the restoration and blessing of Israel's tribes; and the full deliverance of creation's wide domain from the lordship of Satan, the curse of God, and the thralldom of corruption. Such were some of the results. Fierce, therefore, was the struggle of the great enemy of God and man at the cross and at the grave of Christ; violent were the efforts of the strong man to prevent his armor from being taken, and his house from being spoiled, but all in vain. Jesus triumphed, "When the waves of death compassed me, the floods of ungodly men made me afraid; the sorrows of hell compassed me about; the snares of death prevented me; in my distress I called upon the LORD, and cried to my God: and He did hear my voice out of His temple, and my cry did enter into His ears" (2 Samuel 22:5-7). Here was apparent weakness, but real power. The apparently vanquished one became the victor. "Jesus was crucified in weakness, but He liveth by the power of God." Having shed His blood as the victim for sin, He left Himself in the hands of the Father, who, by the eternal Spirit, brought Him again from the dead. He resisted not, but sullied Himself to be trampled upon, and thus crushed the power of the enemy. Satan, by man's agency, nailed Him to the cross, laid Him in the grave, and set a seal upon Him, that He might not rise; but He came up out of the horrible pit, and out of the miry clay, "having spoiled principalities and powers." He went down into the very heart of the enemy's dominion, only that He might make a show of him openly.

From verses 8–20, we have the interference of Jehovah on the part of His righteous servant, set forth in language sublime and powerful beyond expression. The imagery used by the inspired Psalmist is of the most solemn and impressive character. "The earth shook and trembled; the foundations of Heaven moved and shook, because He was wroth. . . . He bowed the heavens also, and came down; and darkness was under His feet. And He rode upon a cherub and did fly; and He was seen upon the wings of the wind. And He made darkness pavilions round about him, dark waters and thick clouds of the skies. . . . The LORD thundered from heaven, and the Most High uttered His voice. And He sent out arrows, and scattered them; lightning, and discomfited them. And the channels of the sea appeared, the foundations of the world were discovered, at the rebuking of the LORD, at the blast of the breath of his nostrils. He sent from above, He took me; He drew me out of many waters." What language is here! Where shall we find anything to equal it? The wrath of the Omnipotent, the thunder of His power, the convulsion of creations entire framework, the artillery of heaven—all these ideas, so glowingly set forward here, outstrip all human imagination. The grave of Christ was the center round which the battle raged in all its fierceness, for there lay the Prince of life. Satan did his utmost; he brought all the power of hell to bear, all "the power of darkness," but he could not hold his captive, because all the claims of justice had been met. The Lord Jesus triumphed over Satan, death, and hell, in strict conformity with the claims of righteousness. This is the sinner's joy, the sinner's peace. It would avail nothing to be told that God over all, blessed forever, had vanquished Satan, a creature of His own creation. But to be told that He, as man's representative, as the sinner's substitute, as the Church's surety, gained the victory, this, when believed, gives the soul ineffable peace; and this is just what the gospel tells us—this is the message which it conveys to the sinner's ear. The apostle tells us that "He (Christ) was delivered for our offences, and raised again for our justification." Having taken upon Himself our sins, and gone down into the grave under the weight of them, resurrection was necessary as the divine proof of His accomplished work. The Holy Spirit, in the gospel, presents Him as risen, ascended, and seated at God's right hand in the heavens, and thus dispels from the believer's heart every doubt, every fear, and every hesitation. "The Lord is risen indeed; His precious blood is new and living wine."

The great argument of the apostle, in 1 Corinthians 15, is based upon this subject. The forgiveness of sins is proved by the resurrection of Christ. "If Christ be not raised, ye are yet in your sins." And, as a consequence, if Christ be raised, ye are not in your sins. Hence, resurrection and forgiveness stand or fall together. Recognize Christ risen, and you recognize sin forgiven. "But now," says the triumphant reasoner, "is Christ risen from the dead, and become the first-fruits of them that slept." This settles all. The moment you take your eye off a risen Christ, you lose the full, deep, divine, peace-giving sense of the forgiveness of sins. The richest fund of experience, the widest range of intelligence will not do as a ground of confidence. Nothing, in short, but JESUS RISEN.

From verses 21-25, we have the ground of Jehovah's interference on behalf of his servant. These verses prove that, in this entire song, we have a greater than David. David could not say, "The LORD rewarded me according to my righteousness; according to the cleanness of my hands hath He recompensed me. For I have kept the ways of the LORD, and have not wickedly departed from my God. For all His judgments were before me; and as for His statutes, I did not depart from them. I was also upright before Him, and have kept myself from mine iniquity. Therefore the LORD hath recompensed me according to my righteousness; according to my cleanness in His eyesight." How different is this language from that of the 51st Psalm, on which we have already dwelt. There it is, "Have mercy upon me, according to thy lovingkindness; according to the multitude of thy tender mercies." This was suitable language for a fallen sinner, as David felt himself to be. He dare not speak of his righteousness, which was as filthy rags; and as to his recompense, he felt that the lake of fire was all that he could, in justice, claim, on the ground of what he was.

Hence, therefore, the language of our chapter is the language of Christ, who alone could use it. He, blessed be His name, could speak of His righteousness, His uprightness, and the cleanness of His hands. And here we see the wondrous grace that shines in redemption. The righteous one took the place of the guilty. "He hath made Him to be sin for us who knew no sin, that we might be made the righteousness of God in Him." Here is the sinner's resting-place. Here he beholds the spotless victim nailed to the cursed tree, *for him;* here he beholds a full redemption flowing from the perfect work of the Lamb of God; here, too, he may behold Jehovah interfering on behalf of his glorious and gracious representative, and, as a consequence, on his behalf, and that, moreover, on strictly righteous grounds. What deep peace this gives to the sin-burdened heart! Deep, ineffable, divine peace!

My reader, if you have not as yet entered into the enjoyment of this peace, let me ask you why have you not? Can you read this chapter with the knowledge of whose language it is, and hesitate, for a moment, to enter into the precious results of the work of a crucified and risen Jesus? Remember, God has left nothing undone to secure your peace; Christ has left nothing undone; and the Holy Spirit bears such a clear and unequivocal testimony in the gospel, as to the perfect salvation that is in Christ Jesus our Lord, that nothing but unbelief can stand in the way. *All has been done.* Precious message! May our hearts delight more and more in it, in the view of all our grievous sins.

David's song closes with a fine allusion to the glories of the latter day, which imparts to it a character of completeness and enlarged compass particularly edifying. "Strangers shall submit themselves unto me." "I will give thanks unto thee among the heathen." Thus are we conducted along a wondrous path, commencing at the cross, and ending in the kingdom. The one who lay in the grave is to sit on the throne; the hand that was pierced with the nail shall wield the scepter; and the brow that was dishonored with a crown of thorns shall be wreathed with a diadem of glory. And never will the top-stone be laid on the superstructure which redeeming love has begun to erect, until the crucified Jesus of Nazareth shall ascend the throne of David, and rule over the house of Jacob. Then shall the glories of redemption be truly celebrated, in heaven and on earth, because the Redeemer shall be exalted, and the redeemed rendered perfectly and eternally happy. We shall then look back, from amid the glories of that bright and happy day, to the cross of the Lord Jesus Christ, as the basis of the whole glorious fabric; and the remembrance of his dying love shall impart fervor and vigor to the song of redemption. "Worthy is the Lamb that was slain to receive power, and riches, and wisdom, and strength, and honor, and glory, and blessing." *Forever*

In David's last words, we learn a similar lesson. It is truly interesting to find, in the history of every servant of God, that having learnt the thorough emptiness of all human and earthly resources, they have fallen back upon God, and found in him an unfailing portion, and a sure refuge. Thus was it with him whose history we have been dwelling upon. Throughout his whole career, he had been learning that divine grace *alone* could meet his need; and, at the close, he gives full expression to this. Whether we look at his "song," or his "last words," the great prominent subject is one and the same —the sufficiency of divine grace.

However, David's last words derive point and energy from the knowledge of God's requirements, in reference to the character of a ruler. "He that ruleth over men must be just, ruling in the fear of God." This is God's standard. Nothing less will do; and where, amongst the ranks of human rulers, shall we find any to come up to it? We may travel down the entire catalogue of those who have occupied the thrones of this world, and not find so much as one who could answer to the two great characteristics set forth in the above comprehensive verse. He must be just, and he must rule in the fear of God.

Psalm 82 furnishes us with the divine challenge of all those who have been set in places of authority. "God standeth in the congregation of the mighty; He judgeth among the gods." What does He find? Justice and the fear of His name? No, far from it "How long will ye judge unjustly, and accept the persons of the wicked?" Such is man. They know not, neither *will* they understand; they walk on in darkness; all the foundations of earth are out of course. What, then, is the resource, in the view of such a humiliating state of things? "Arise, O God, judge the earth; for thou shalt inherit all nations." The Lord Jesus is here presented as the one alone competent to fill the throne according to the thoughts of God, and Psalm 72 gives us a lovely picture of what His government will be. "He shall judge thy people with righteousness, and thy poor with judgment." "He shall judge the poor of the people, he shall save the children of the needy, and shall break in pieces the oppressor." "He shall come down like rain upon the mown grass; as showers that water the earth." In short, the entire psalm must be read as a sample of the millennial kingdom of the Son of Man, and the reader will perceive how entirely David's last words harmonize with the spirit of it. "And he shall be as the light of the morning, when the sun riseth, even a morning without clouds; as the tender grass springeth out of the earth by clear shining after rain. Truly refreshing and soul-reviving is this! And how does the heart rejoice to turn away from the dark and dreary scene through which we are passing, to contemplate "a morning without clouds." There is no morning now without a cloud. How could there be? How could a fallen race, a groaning world, enjoy a cloudless sky? Impossible, until the atoning efficacy of the cross shall have been applied to all, and the whole creation shall have entered into its full repose beneath the shadow of Immanuel's wings.

Look where you will, and clouds and darkness meet your view. A groaning creation, a scattered Israel, a broken church, perverted systems, false profession, corrupt principles. All these things tend, like the smoke of the bottomless pit, to darken the horizon around us, and obscure our vision. But, how the heart bounds at the thought of the morning without clouds! Well might the Psalmist call it "a clear shining after rain." The children of God have ever felt this world to be a place of clouds and rain, a vale of tears; but the millennial morning will put a period to all this: its rising sun will disperse the clouds, and God Himself shall wipe away all tears from their faces. Bright and happy prospect! Blessed be the grace that has set it before us, and the atoning work which has secured our title to it!

But it has been remarked, that no human office bearer ever came up to the divine standard, as set forth in David's last words. David himself felt this. "MY house is not so with God." Such was his humble, soul-subduing sense of what he was. We have already seen how fully, how deeply, how unaffectedly, he entered into the vast distance between what he was *personally* and the divine requirement, when he exclaimed, "*I* was born in sin;" "*Thou* desirest truth in the inward parts." His experience was the same when he looked at himself *officially*. "My house is not so with God." Neither as *a man,* nor as *a king,* was he what he ought to be. And hence it was that grace was so precious to his heart. He looked into the mirror of God's perfect law, and saw therein his own deformity; he then turned round and looked at God's "covenant, ordered in *all* things and *sure,*" and here he rested with unquestioning simplicity. Though David's house was not ordered in all things, yet God's covenant was, and David could, therefore, say, "This is all my salvation, and all my desire." He had learnt to look away from himself and his house straight to God, and His everlasting covenant. And, we may say, that just as his apprehension of his own personal and official nothingness was deep and real, would his sense of what grace had done for him be deep and real also. The view of what God was had humbled him; the view of what God was had lifted him up. It was his joy, as he traveled to the end of all human things, to find his resting-place in the blessed covenant of his God, in which he found embodied, and eternally secured, all his salvation and all his desire.

How blessed it is, dear reader, to find thus our *all* in God! not merely to use Him as one who makes up our deficiency, or the deficiency of human objects, but to make Him our all; to use Him as one who supersedes every one and everything, in our estimation. This is what we want. God must be set above all, not merely in reference to the forgiveness of sins, but also in reference to our every necessity. "I am God, and there is none else." "Look unto ME."

There are many who can trust God for salvation, who, nevertheless, fail much in the minute details of life; and yet God is glorified in being made the depositary of all our cares, and the bearer of all our burdens. There is nothing too small to be brought to Him, and nothing so small as not to be more than a match for our capacity, did we but enter into the sense of our nothingness.

But we find another element in this 23rd chapter, an element, too, which might seem introduced rather abruptly: I

allude to the record of David's mighty men. This has been already alluded to; but it is interesting to notice it in connection with God's covenant.

There were two things to cheer and comfort David's heart; the faithfulness of God, and the devotedness of his servants. And, in looking at the close of Paul's course, we find that he had the same springs of comfort and encouragement. In the second epistle to Timothy, he glances at the condition of things around him; he sees the "great house," which assuredly was not so with God as he required it; he sees all that were in Asia turned away from him; he sees Hymeneus and Philetus teaching false doctrine, and overturning the faith of some; he sees Alexander the coppersmith doing much mischief; he sees many with itching ears, heaping to themselves teachers, and turning away from the truth to fables; he sees the perilous times setting in with fearful rapidity: in a word, he sees the whole fabric, humanly speaking, going to pieces; but he, like David, rested in the assurance that "the foundation of God standeth sure," and he was also cheered by the individual devotedness of some mighty man or other, who, through the grace of God, was standing faithful amid the wreck. He remembered the faith of a Timothy, the love of an Onesiphorus; and, moreover, he was cheered by the fact that in darkest times there would be a company of faithful ones who would call on the Lord out of a pure heart. These latter he exhorts Timothy to follow, having purged himself from the dishonorable vessels of the great house.

Thus was it with David. He could count his worthies, and record their deeds. Though his own house was not what it ought to be, and though "the sons of Belial" were around him, yet he could speak of an Adino, a Dodo, and a Shammah, men who had hazarded their lives for him, and signalized their names by deeds of prowess against the uncircumcised.

Thank God, He will never leave Himself without a witness; He will always have a people devoted to His cause in the world. Did we not know and believe this, at a time like the present, our hearts might, indeed, sink within us. A few years have wrought a mighty change in the sphere of action of many Christians. Things are not as they once were amongst us, and we may with truth say, "Our house is not so with God." Many of us have, it may be, been disappointed; we looked for much, and, alas! it has come to little. We have found that we were just like others, or, if we differed, it was in our making a higher profession, and, as a consequence, incurring higher responsibilities, and exhibiting greater inconsistencies. We thought we were somewhat, but we grievously erred, and are now learning our error. The Lord grant that we may learn it rightly, learn it thoroughly, learn it in the dust, in His presence, that so we may never lift up our heads again, but walk in the abiding sense of our own emptiness. The Lord's address to Laodicea may be used with profit, "Because thou sayest, I am rich, and increased with goods, and have need of nothing; and knowest not that thou art wretched, and miserable, and poor, and blind, and naked: I counsel thee to buy of me gold tried in the fire, that thou mayest be rich; and white raiment, that thou mayest he clothed, and that the shame of thy nakedness do not appear; and anoint thine eyes with eyesalve, that thou mayest see."

If our past experience leads us to cling more simply to Jesus, we shall have reason to bless the Lord for it all; and, as it is, we cannot but feel it to be a special mercy to be delivered from every false ground of confidence. If we were seeking to build up a system, it is well to be delivered from its influence and to be brought to adhere simply to the Word and Spirit of God, which are the appointed companions of the Church's path through the wilderness.

Nor are we, either, void of the sweet encouragement to be derived from the devotedness of one or another here and there. There are many who are proving their affection for the Person of Christ, and the high estimation in which they hold the doctrine of the Church. This is a great mercy. The enemy, though he has done much mischief, has it not all his own way. There are those who are ready to spend their strength and energy in the defense of the gospel. May the Lord add to their number; may He also add to the vigor of their testimony; and, finally, may He make us increasingly thankful for His grace in having set before us, in His Word, the true position and path of His servants in these last days, and, also, those principles which can alone sustain us in the midst of the abounding strife and confusion. All we need expect is to be kept faithful to the end. If we are seeking to make a noise in the world, or raise a testimony, we shall be disappointed; but if we are content to walk humbly with our God, we shall have reason to rejoice, and our labor shall not be in vain.

David had thought to do much in his day, and was sincere in the thought; but he had to learn that the will of God concerning him was, that he should "serve his generation." We, too, must learn this; we must learn that an humble mind, a devoted heart, a tender conscience, an honest purpose, are far more precious in the sight of God than mere outward services, however showy and attractive. "To obey is better than sacrifice; and to hearken than the fat of rams." Salutary words, these, for a day of religiousness, like the present, wherein divine principle is so loosely held.

The Lord keep us faithful to the end, so that whether, like those who have gone before us, we fall asleep in Jesus, or be caught up to meet Him in the air, we "may be found of Him in peace, without spot, and blameless." Meanwhile, let us rejoice in the apostle's word to his son Timothy, "The foundation of

God standeth sure, having this seal, The Lord knoweth them that are His; and, Let every one that nameth the name of Christ depart from iniquity."

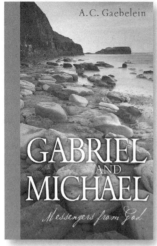
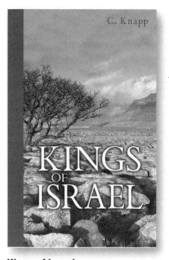
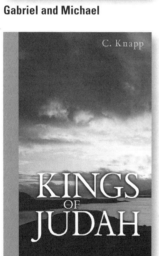
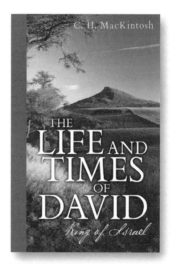

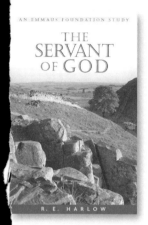
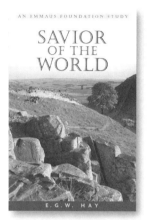
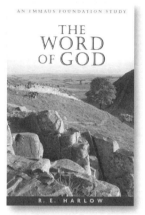
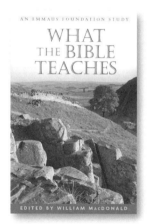
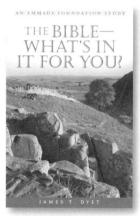

A DEVOTIONAL COMMENTARY

Genesis
From Creation
to a Nation